Christmas

The Annual of Christmas Literature and Art

Christmas

O Tannenbaum

O Tannenbaum, O Tannenbaum,

Wie treu sind deine Blätter!

Du grünst nicht nur zur Sommerzeit,

Nein auch im Winter, wenn es schneit.

O Tannenbaum, O Tannenbaum,

Wie treu sind deine Blätter!

Christmas
The Annual of Christmas Literature and Art

Volume Sixty

Augsburg Fortress, Minneapolis

Table of Contents

In this volume

Among the many traditions that have worked their way into the American observance of Christmas, the festooned and illustrated evergreen stands foremost in our homes and in our hearts. It is to that glowing symbol of the yuletide that we dedicate this volume of CHRISTMAS.

Acknowledging the German origin of the Christmas tree, the frontispiece on page two features the well-known carol "O Tannenbaum" rendered in the ancient art of fraktur.

The article "Legends and Lore of the Yuletide Tree" by Suzanne Campbell brings to light the often shadowy history of the Christmas tree. In "The Decorated Tree" Philip Rulon describes and Betty Sievert illustrates five distinct styles of ornamentation practiced in regions of the United States.

Tree farmer Marvin Thrasher gives an inside look at the trees that grace our homes in "Growing a Holiday Tradition," while artist Bob Artley looks back at cherished holiday celebrations in "Christmas Trees Remembered."

Along a somewhat different vein, "The Tree of Jesse" by Phillip Gugel explores the portrayal in religious art of Jesus' family tree. The article showcases a variety of examples from medieval times to the present.

What many would consider another art form is described in the article by doll collector Audrey Teeple, "American Cloth Dolls." Many children have awakened on Christmas morning to find a handmade doll under the tree. Illustrated with photos of prized dolls from various collectors, the article tells the stories of talented women who turned their love for dolls into prosperous cottage industries.

Other highlights of this volume include a short story by Walter Wangerin; a photo-essay on the Moravian settlement of Bethlehem, Pennsylvania, by Tim Gilman; and an historic look at four favorite American carols.

Opening the book, the exquisite drawings of Peter Church convey the beauty and grace of the biblical account of Jesus' birth. May that story be your cause for celebration this and every Christmas season.

Editorial staff: Gloria E. Bengtson, Jennifer Huber, Sandra Gangelhoff, Carol Evans-Smith. Advisory committee: Carol Erdahl, M. Alexandra George, Mary Lohre, Cynthia Nelson, Lewann Sotnak.

The Christmas Story

According to St. Luke and St. Matthew

And it came to pass in those days that a decree went out from Caesar Augustus that all the world should be registered. This census first took place while Quirinius was governing Syria. So all went to be registered, everyone to his own city.

And Joseph also went up from Galilee, out of the city of Nazareth, into Judea, to the city of David, which is called Bethlehem, because he was of the house and lineage of David, to be registered with Mary, his betrothed wife, who was with Child.

So it was, that while they were there, the days were completed for her to be delivered.

And she brought forth her firstborn Son, and wrapped Him in swaddling cloths, and laid Him in a manger, because there was no room for them in the inn.

Now there were in the same country shepherds living out in the fields, keeping watch over their flock by night. And behold, an angel of the Lord stood before them, and the glory of the Lord shone around them, and they were greatly afraid.

Then the angel said to them, "Do not be afraid, for behold, I bring you good tidings of great joy which will be to all people. For there is born to you this day in the city of David a Savior, who is Christ the Lord. And this will be the sign to you: You will find a Babe wrapped in swaddling cloths, lying in a manger."

And suddenly there was with the angel a multitude of the heavenly host praising God and saying:

"Glory to God in the highest,
And on earth peace, good will toward men!"

7

o it was, when the angels had gone away from them into heaven, that the shepherds said to one another, "Let us now go to Bethlehem and see this thing that has come to pass, which the Lord has made known to us."

And they came with haste and found Mary and Joseph, and the Babe lying in a manger. Now when they had seen Him, they made widely known the saying which was told them concerning this child. And all those who heard it marveled at those things which were told them by the shepherds. But Mary kept all these things and pondered them in her heart. Then the shepherds returned, glorifying and praising God for all the things that they had heard and seen, as it was told them.

9

ow after Jesus was born in Bethlehem of Judea in the days of Herod the king, behold, wise men from the East came to Jerusalem, saying, "Where is He who has been born King of the Jews? For we have seen His star in the East and have come to worship Him."

When Herod the king heard these things, he was troubled, and all Jerusalem with him. And when he had gathered all the chief priests and scribes of the people together, he inquired of them where the Christ was to be born.

So they said to him, "In Bethlehem of Judea, for thus it is written by the prophet:

'But you, Bethlehem, in the land of Judah,
Are not the least among the rulers of Judah;
For out of you shall come a Ruler
Who will shepherd My people Israel.'"

Then Herod, when he had secretly called the wise men, determined from them what time the star appeared. And he sent them to Bethlehem and said, "Go and search diligently for the young Child, and when you have found Him, bring back word to me, that I may come and worship Him also."

When they heard the king, they departed;
and behold, the star which they had seen in
the East went before them, till it came and stood
over where the young Child was. When they
saw the star, they rejoiced with exceedingly
great joy.

And when they had come into the house,
they saw the young Child with Mary His
mother, and fell down and worshiped Him.
And when they had opened their treasures,
they presented gifts to Him: gold, frankincense,
and myrrh.

Then, being divinely warned in a dream that
they should not return to Herod, they departed
for their own country another way.

ow when they had departed, behold, an angel of the Lord appeared to Joseph in a dream, saying, "Arise, take the young Child and His mother, flee to Egypt, and stay there until I bring you word; for Herod will seek the young Child to destroy Him."

When he arose, he took the young Child and His mother by night and departed for Egypt, and was there until the death of Herod, that it might be fulfilled which was spoken by the Lord through the prophet, saying, "Out of Egypt I called My Son."

But when Herod was dead, behold, an angel of the Lord appeared in a dream to Joseph in Egypt, saying, "Arise, take the young Child and His mother, and go to the land of Israel, for those who sought the young Child's life are dead."

Then he arose, took the young Child and His mother, and came into the land of Israel. But when he heard that Archelaus was reigning over Judea instead of his father Herod, he was afraid to go there. And being warned by God in a dream, he turned aside into the region of Galilee.

And he came and dwelt in a city called Nazareth, that it might be fulfilled which was spoken by the prophets, "He shall be called a Nazarene."

Legends and Lore of the Yuletide Tree

SUZANNE P. CAMPBELL

BITTER DECEMBER WINDS howled through northern Europe and ice crystals drove like needles into the faces of the eighth-century Druids. It was the season of the winter solstice, the time when the "sun stands still." Nights were long and dark; the sun god had lost his power. The Druids huddled together in rude huts and placed evergreen boughs around the doors to protect themselves against the demons that they believed were liberated at this time of year. Because its foliage never withered and fell, the evergreen represented life and thus was believed to overpower darkness and death. Even Odin, Norse god of thunder, was transformed into a demon during this season of the yuletide festival. Blood sacrifices were made beneath his sacred oak to propitiate him and great fires were lit to strengthen and call back the waning sun.

Into this frozen land came a Christmas missionary, Wilfred of Crediton, later called St. Boniface. Though no one knows where the first Christmas tree was erected, many chronicles attribute its origin to him. As German legend has it, Wilfred determined to destroy a sacred oak in which the people believed Odin dwelt and beneath whose branches blood sacrifices were made. Upon his first blow the tree split into four parts and crashed to the ground. There, just behind it, stood a small fir tree. Wilfred proclaimed this unsullied young tree the symbol of the new Christian faith.

He let the axe drop and said to the astonished Druids who had come to watch the feat, "This little tree, a child of the forest, shall be your holy tree tonight. It is a wood of peace, for your houses are built of the fir. It is a sign of endless life, for its leaves are ever green. See

how it points upward to heaven! Let this be called the tree of the Christ child. Take it up and carry it to the chieftain's hall. You shall go no more into the shadows of the forest to keep your feasts with secret rites of shame. You shall keep them at home with laughter and songs and rites of love, gathered around the green fir tree to rejoice in the birth night of Christ. Gather about the tree, not in the wildwood but in your homes. There it will shelter no deeds of blood, but loving gifts and acts of kindness and brotherhood."

Other legends of the yuletide tree stretch back to creation itself. Many believed that the fir was the Tree of Life that grew in the garden of Eden and from which Eve picked the forbidden fruit. After the deed its foliage and flowers shrank to needles, only to bloom again on the night of Jesus' birth.

Generations of believers would tell stories of the miracles that happened that holy night: Every tree in the forest, no matter how bare and black of branch, sprang into full flower, fruit, and leaf. The balsam gardens of Engedi on the shore of the Dead Sea burst into full bloom, wrapping the little village of Bethlehem in their scent. When the shepherds on the hillside heard the glad news they were amazed to see the tiny, starlike blossoms of the rose of Jericho unfurl its petals beneath their feet, having sprung from the footprints of Mary, who had passed that way earlier. By the roadside a rosemary bush flowered blue, not its accustomed white, because it had been brushed by the virgin's cloak.

In Medieval Europe

One ancient Christian tradition associated with the evergreen as a Christmas tree concerns the medieval miracle plays. Since few people in medieval Europe could read, miracle plays were presented outside the churches as a way to dramatize scriptural stories and thereby teach the congregation. Fourteenth- and seventeenth-century church calendars listed December 24 as Adam and Eve's Day. Naturally, this was the time when a play concerning the story of the fruit tree in the Garden of Eden would be presented.

Imagine yourself in the square of a small European village in the dead of winter. A stage stands at the center of the square, bare except for a magnificent fir tree hung with glowing red apples. A ring of lighted candles surrounds and illuminates the tree. Often, the character playing Adam would parade through the streets of the village before the performance carrying a small version of this "Paradise tree." Since there were no apple trees in fruit at the time, an evergreen decorated with apples was the usual substitute.

In time the symbol of the tree, the only stage prop used in the play, made a strong impression on the worshipers watching the performance. By the seventeenth century it no longer represented just the Tree of Life or the sin of temptation but became rather a symbol of the nativity. As late as the nineteenth century, however, people in Northern Germany still purchased little figures of Adam, Eve, and the serpent to put under their "Tree of Life."

The earliest historical references to the Christmas tree appear in the sixteenth century and come from Latvia and Estonia, now parts of the Soviet Union. Riga and Revel, both Baltic port cities, recorded tree ceremonies in the early 1500s. Members of the local merchants guild dressed formally in black hats and carried evergreen trees festooned with artificial roses to the marketplace. There, in a seeming vestige of paganism, they danced around the trees then set them on fire.

The German Contribution

It is the Germans who can be credited with developing the Christmas tree tradition as we know it today. In 1531 Christmas trees were sold at the Strasbourg market in Alsace (which was then a German territory but is now in France). The trees were set up in local homes for the holiday but remained undecorated. Evidently the practice was quite common, for a local ordinance passed in Ammerschweier (also in Alsace) stated that no person "shall have for Christmas more than one bush of more than eight shoe lengths," which would have been about four feet tall. Nearby districts had ordinances that prohibited the taking of any greens for the holiday.

A 1605 diary fragment left by an unknown Frenchman

is the oldest known reference to a decorated Christmas tree: "At Christmas they set up fir trees in the parlor at Strasbourg and hang thereon roses cut out of many-colored paper, apples, wafers, gold foil and sweets." In early Christian art the rose symbolized the Virgin Mary and the wafers represented the communion host and therefore Christ.

Because the use of the evergreen as a symbol of fertility was so deeply ingrained in European pagan culture, the Catholic church frequently banned or discouraged its use. In the 1640s theologian Johann Konrad Dannahauer of Strasbourg wrote, "Among other trifles which are set up during Christmastime instead of God's word, is the Christmas tree or fir tree, which is put up at home and decorated with dolls and sugar." But the age-old custom continued and the tree was eventually transformed into a Christmas symbol.

By the seventeenth century the evergreen, ancient symbol of life, had become a familiar sight in Christian homes during the Christmas season. A tree decorated with wafers or cookies representing the communion host became known as a *Christbaum* (Christ tree) and these appeared in a number of forms during the seventeenth and eighteenth centuries. Sometimes the trees were hung upside-down from the rafters and decorated with red paper, apples, or gilded nuts. Others were suspended from windows or rafters, right side up with an apple stuck on the sharpened point of the trunk.

In Germany, about the same time that the candleless Christbaum was becoming popular, another Christmas custom arose. This was the erection of a *lichtstock*, an open wooden pyramid with shelves on which candles were placed. The candle was a powerful religious symbol of Jesus Christ as the Light of the world. The lichtstock was often decorated by winding evergreen branches around each leg of the pyramid and placing a star or acorn at the apex. Little gifts were placed on the tiny shelves. Though not a tree at all it's easy to see why some regard the lichtstock as the great grandparent of the modern Christmas tree. It was adopted by the English, Welsh, and Italians, who each added their own touches. German families of the seventeenth century often placed the glowing lichtstock beside their undecorated Christbaum on the night before Christmas.

Martin Luther is credited by many scholars with the creation of the first lighted Christmas tree. He was said to have been so enchanted with the splendor of the stars one Christmas Eve that he adorned a fir tree with candles to symbolize Christ as the Light of the world and presented the little tree to his children.

The first historical evidence of a lighted Christmas tree

appears more than a century after Luther's death in 1546. It comes from a sister-in-law of Louis XIV of France. In 1708, Liselotte von der Pfalz described in a letter the Christmas trees she remembered from her childhood in Germany: "Tables are fixed up like altars and outfitted for each child with all sorts of things, such as new clothes, silver, dolls, sugar candy, and so forth. Boxwood trees are set on the tables, and a candle is fastened to each branch."

The Christmas tree was introduced in France by Princess Helen of Mecklenburg in 1837 after her marriage to the Duke of Orleans. Four years later, Queen Victoria's German husband, Prince Albert, popularized the Christmas tree tradition in England in celebration of the birth of their first son. His was not the first English Christmas tree, however. Dr. John Watkins, a member of the court

of Queen Charlotte, Victoria's grandmother and the consort of George III, described a Christmas tree at Windsor Castle in 1800. "In the middle of the room stood an immense tub with a yew tree placed in it, from the branches of which hung bunches of sweetmeats, almonds, and raisins in papers, fruits, and toys, most tastefully arranged, and the whole illuminated by small wax candles."

But Albert was such an enthusiastic advocate, and the Victorians were so fond of imitating the royal household, the custom spread rapidly. Albert presented decorated

trees to schools and army barracks, as well as seeing to it that the royal family had a richly decorated tree each year. Their candlelit tree was covered with expensive sweets contained in elegant baskets and trays. On the top stood a small angel with outstretched wings, holding a wreath in each hand.

The angel was probably a copy of the famous Nuremberg angel. Legend has it that a German dollmaker made the first one in memory of his beloved daughter, who had been killed during the Thirty Years' War that raged throughout Europe from 1618-1648. Though Victoria kept all of Albert's possessions until her own death in 1901, the little angel along with all of the other tree ornaments has since mysteriously disappeared.

In Germany and America the Christmas tree was further popularized in the early twentieth century by accounts in newspapers and magazines of the German royal family's holiday traditions. Every year the kaiser decorated table trees at his palace in Potsdam for every member of his immediate family. Each tree was sized appropriately for its recipient. At one time he did 12, one each for himself, his wife, six sons, three daughters, and one grandchild.

The most important thing Germany ever exported was Christmas. It gave the world the small tabletop Christmas tree alight with candles.

The most important thing Germany ever exported was Christmas, it's been said. Indeed it was Germany that shared with the world the custom of the small tabletop Christmas tree decorated with imagination and alight with candles. It was the American people, however, who introduced the floor-standing tree whose branches swept the ceiling.

The American Christmas Tree

The first reference to a large Christmas tree that stood on the floor appeared in the December 1860 issue of *Godey's Lady's Book:* "The square of green baize being tacked down, a large stone jar was placed in the middle of it, and in this the tree stood nobly erect. Damp sand was put around the stem till the large green tree stood firmly in place. A flounce of green chintz round the jar concealed its stony ugliness, and over the top, round the tree, was a soft cushion of moss. It was a large evergreen, reaching almost to the ceiling, for all the family presents were to be placed under it." The decorations had changed by then too and were no longer concentrated on the edible but rather ornaments that could be kept from year to year. One popular choice was the new glass Christmas ball being imported from Germany. But we must go back 150 years if we want to see how the Christmas tree first came to America.

The Christmas tree entered America as the cherished companion of German settlers from the Rhine provinces. They were part of the first wave of German immigration about 1700. These Pennsylvania Dutch immigrants (*Dutch* is a corruption of *Deutsch*, meaning "German") made their homes in south central Pennsylvania. By 1820 decorated trees were fairly common in the larger towns of the region and within two decades the custom had spread to the small villages.

The area beneath the tree was as important as the tree itself to the Pennsylvania Dutch. It was reserved for the *putz* or manger scene. The first putzes were created by the Moravians who had settled around the town of Bethlehem, Pennsylvania. In preparation for Christmas, moss was dug up and replanted in cellars during November. At Christmas it was used as a carpet around the tree trunk on which the manger scene was arranged. Rocks, twigs, and other natural ornaments surrounded the creche containing the clay figures of Mary, Joseph, the baby Jesus, and the animals of the stable.

Four hundred years passed between the creation of the first "Paradise trees" and the American invention of the electric Christmas tree light by Thomas Edison in 1910.

The custom of Christmas began to spread more widely. In 1836, Alabama became the first state to declare Christmas a legal holiday; Louisiana and Arkansas followed. Despite that early support, the decorated Christmas tree caught on slowly in the South. In 1851 Mahalia Eggleston Roach, a niece of Jefferson Davis, who lived on a plantation in Mississippi wrote in her diary, "The children had such a number of gifts that I made a Christmas tree for them. Mother, aunt, and Liz came down to see it; all said it was something new to them. I never saw one, but learned from some of the German stories I had been reading."

By 1890 December 25 was declared a legal holiday in all U.S. states and territories. The Christmas tree itself had become so popular by 1889 that President Benjamin Harrison caused four generations of his family members to assemble around the White House tree. He expressed the hope that their example of having an old-fashioned Christmas tree would be followed by every family in the land. In 1912, the first Christmas tree was erected in Madison Square in New York. This introduced a new custom, the erection of lighted trees in public places. The practice was enthusiastically adopted throughout the U.S. and introduced to Europe after World War I where it became even more popular after World War II.

Four hundred years passed between the creation of the first "Paradise trees" and the American invention of the electric Christmas tree light by Thomas Edison in 1910. Now illuminated trees were safe as well as beautiful. Perhaps Edison got the idea from Edgar Gribble,

chief electrician of the Palace Hotel in San Francisco.

Gribble is credited with having decorated the first electrically lighted Christmas tree there in 1896. During Christmas 1897 one reporter wrote, "It is set up for the pleasure of the guests in the courtyard and is the biggest tree in the city. It is forty feet high and was brought specially from Marin County on two flatcars of the North Pacific Coast Company. On its branches the chief electrician, Edgar Gribble, has strung 500 electric lights. The globes are of five different colors and the effect is gorgeous. The lights look like brilliant fruit growing on the mammoth tree."

And so, wrenched from its birth as a symbol of the pagan fear of darkness and of death, the evergreen has come to symbolize rebirth and everlasting life. At its foot no longer lay the blood sacrifices of Druids terrified of vengeful gods, but the creche—figures of the holy infant, Mary, Joseph, the shepherds filled with wonder, and the Magi bringing gifts.

There lies the true meaning of Christmas: perfect love casts out all fear. And the glowing tree embodies the scriptural message that inspired its origin: *Lumen Christi*—the Light of Christ.

The Christmas City, U.S.A.

TIM GILMAN

EACH DECEMBER Bethlehem, Pennsylvania, transforms itself into the Christmas City, U.S.A. Thousands of holiday lights adorn hundreds of trees. Thousands of single electric candles light the windows of hundreds of homes and businesses. Thousands of visitors arrive on hundreds of charter buses to marvel at the huge Star of Bethlehem overlooking this eastern Pennsylvania city. Not only is the story of Christmas celebrated, but the story of Bethlehem, which dates back nearly three centuries, is told by costumed guides.

A Moravian Settlement

Founded in 1741, Bethlehem became the first permanent settlement in North America of the Moravian Church. For more than 100 years it was a "closed community" for these Czech-German Protestant missionaries. Only Moravians could be residents and own land in the church-controlled community.

The Moravian Church, the popular name for the *Unitas Fratrum* (Unity of Brethren) in the English-speaking world, originated in 1457 with Hussite reformers in Bohemia (present-day Czechoslovakia). After almost 200 years of expansion into nearby Moravia and Poland, the Thirty Years' War and the ensuing Protestant persecution forced the brethren underground. These pre-Reformation Protestants later migrated from Moravia (Czechoslovakia) to nearby Saxony (East Germany) and re-established themselves as the Renewed Unitas Fratrum.

The Moravians forged a solid foundation of customs and traditions. It is upon this foundation that Bethlehem built its heritage. Even after 250 years, the community of 71,000 Bethlehemites recognizes the value of the Moravian Church in its city's history and looks to the church's traditions and customs as mainstays of the holiday season celebration.

As with most Christian denominations, Christmas is a time of major celebration for Moravians. Among the pillars of faith in the Moravian Church are the convictions that the person of Jesus Christ is the central figure and the Scriptures are the final authority. Thus the Moravians embrace the birth and the death of the Savior Jesus as the two main events around which their religious calendar revolves.

In 1937 Christmas in Bethlehem took on added significance as the Christmas City, U.S.A., concept was born. The president of the Chamber of Commerce, Vernon K. Melhado, recognized the uniqueness of Bethlehem's heritage and sought to incorporate it into a citywide Christmas program for the town's citizens and visitors. Melhado, a Presbyterian, made a radio appeal to the community that Bethlehem become the "Christmas City of the United States."

The city's inaugural Christmas lighting ceremony followed and 22 city blocks were bathed in brilliant holiday decorations. A community *putz* or manger scene was erected for the first time that year. The Christmas city idea was an instant success and thousands came to see the new holiday attraction.

Christmas Lights

Today the Christmas City, U.S.A., has been refined to a more dignified and less lavish holiday celebration. Simple white lights have replaced the varicolored bulbs and large decorative holiday objects, such as glass stars and assorted ornamental objects. More than 600 trees, both evergreen and deciduous, are decorated with strings of lights. Many small Christmas trees are fastened to light standards along major streets and intersections.

Bethlehem's Christmas season begins on the

The Bethlehem Plaza glistens with Christmas decorations after a winter rain. Bethlehem was founded in 1741, and became the "Christmas City of the United States" in 1937.

first weekend of Advent. A flick of the master switch at the Christmas City Lighting Ceremony that Sunday evening illuminates the citywide presentation of 65,000 lights. Several 15-foot Advent displays are lit by the first of four large candles, one for each Sunday preceding Christmas. The community tree, a 40- to 50-foot evergreen customarily donated by a city resident, dwarfs smaller lighted trees on the Hill-to-Hill Bridge that links north and south Bethlehem. High atop South Mountain shines the 91-foot Star of Bethlehem, which serves as a beacon for the Christmas season.

The star is the crown jewel in the city's lighting display, although it was first erected in 1935 before the Christmas City fanfare. Perched on South Mountain, the 91-foot steel structure is the largest of its kind in the world and can be seen from 20 miles away. The two faces of the star, north and south, are illuminated by 246 bulbs. The five-point star is actually 20 feet in diameter with large emanating rays.

The star was selected as the focal point of the official city emblem. The points stand for five major areas of interest to its citizenry—education, religion, music, recreation, and industry.

The first weekend of Advent also signals the start of a busy holiday season calendar compiled by the Bethlehem Area Chamber of Commerce, which continues the leadership role it assumed in establishing the Christmas City program in 1937. A chamber-sponsored Community Advent Breakfast is held Saturday for the secular and clerical leaders of the city to welcome the holiday season. Later in the day a family Christmas tree decorating party takes place at the City Center Complex.

The Christmas Tour and Information Center, operated by the chamber at a convenient downtown location, opens to assist both residents and visitors. It serves as a starting point for the popular Night Light Tours, during which an escort in traditional eighteenth-century Moravian dress points out Bethlehem's holiday and historic sites during the one-hour bus tour. The visitors are awed by the citywide lighting, which is said to be the largest display for a city the size of Bethlehem. The panoramic view of the Christmas City with its glittering decorations from the top of South Mountain is breathtaking, especially as part of a Night Light Tour.

The chamber estimates that as many as 50,000 visitors have made the annual pilgrimage to Christmas City, U.S.A., in recent years. Many of these come on tour buses from as far away as Ohio, Georgia, Maine, and Ontario, Canada.

The momentous task of maintaining the holiday lighting is the responsibility of the city's electrical department. The Chamber of Commerce finances the lighting through the sale of Christmas City seals. The year 1989 marked the twenty-fifth anniversary of the popular stamp-like seals that residents affix to their holiday mail. A photograph of the Star of Bethlehem was aptly chosen to grace the seal.

Collectors covet the Christmas City seals, especially the limited issue cachet envelopes which are canceled with a special Christmas City, U.S.A., postmark. The Bethlehem postmaster reports that more than 200,000 pieces of mail, including numerous requests from philatelists, are hand-canceled with one of two Christmas City postmarks.

Light is also an essential part of the Moravian commemoration of Christ's birth. The universal Christian conviction that Jesus is the Light of the world is expressed by Moravians with the single lit candle and the Moravian star. Moravians in Bethlehem place a candle in every window. The historic Moravian buildings and many residences glow with these simple white lights. Even businesses and non-Moravians have adopted this practice, which commences the First Sunday in Advent and beautifully complements the city's lighting program.

Young Moravian soloist for "Morning Star" holds a lighted beeswax candle trimmed with red flameproof tissue paper.

The Moravians begin the holiday season with an Advent lovefeast service on Sunday morning. The custom of the lovefeast originated in 1727 when Count Zinzendorf sent food to the Moravian worshipers to whom he had given refuge on his Saxony estate five years earlier. That service marked the reemergence of the Moravian brethren as the Renewed Unitas Fratrum after 100 years of severe religious persecution.

Bishop John de Watteville's Christmas Eve lovefeast of 1747 firmly established the practice of sharing food and drink during the service as an act of fellowship patterned after the early Christian agape meal. Today the lovefeast is reserved for such special religious observances as Advent and Christmas. A simple fare of coffee (chocolate milk for the children) and a sweet bun is generally served in Bethlehem congregations. Some Moravian congregations hold a separate candlelight lovefeast for children prior to the Christmas Eve vigils, while others combine the two.

The beeswax candle is the common choice among North American Moravians. Beeswax is the purest form of wax and symbolizes the purity of Christ. The taper burns clean and slow with minimal wax run-off, making it very suitable for hand holding. A pleasant aroma is emitted from the bright yellow to tannish colored wax.

Candlemaking in Bethlehem is an important practice in order to supply the large demand for beeswax tapers during the holiday season. Beeswax candlemaking and trimming demonstrations are given regularly at the 1762 Waterworks building in the eighteenth-century industrial area, adjacent to the downtown.

A tradition unique to the Unitas Fratrum brethren is the multi-pointed, three-dimensional Moravian star. It is sometimes called the Advent star as it is often hung with internal illumination on the First Sunday in Advent.

The customary geometric configuration of 26 points dates back to about 1850 when it was first made during handcraft sessions of the Moravian boys boarding school in Niesky, Germany, near Herrnhut. An alumnus, Peter Verbeek, began producing the stars commercially from his home. His son later founded the Herrnhut Star Factory, which produced the popular stars for decades until war closed the plant. Today stars are made again in Herrnhut and are often called the *Herrnhuter Adventstern* on the European continent where Moravians are known as Herrnhuters after their town of origin.

The white star is the choice in Bethlehem. Many homes and businesses hang a star in a window or entrance during the Christmas season. Most Moravian churches suspend a star in the sanctuary during the holiday season. One of the largest in Bethlehem is a yellow six-foot 26-point star that hangs in the Central Moravian Church from the First Sunday in Advent until Epiphany. A few congregations display the "magnificent" 110-point star, also of Niesky design. Such stars grace the Lititz, Pennsylvania, and Herrnhut churches.

Stars and beeswax candles are among the most popular gift items lining the shelves of the downtown shopping district during the holiday season. Moravian mints and Moravian sugar cake are favorites, too. White holiday lights strung on trees combine with the Victorian gas lamps to entice shoppers along historic Main Street. Many of the quaint shops and businesses along Main Street have restored their Victorian facades to complement the late nineteenth century restoration of the street begun more than a decade ago.

Putzing

The "Light of the world" shines brightly through another somewhat unique Moravian custom—the *putz*. Stemming from the German word *putzen*, which means "to decorate," a putz is a miniature landscape that portrays the nativity story with biblical figurines and animals.

The traditional Christian creche is the focal point of the tableau, which also illustrates the series of major events leading to the birth of the Christ child. The display has no bounds and is situated at the foot of a Christmas tree, on a fireplace mantle, or on a room-size platform.

Gathering the material and assembling the putz is often a family affair. A late fall trip is made to collect the moss,

(above) The Moravian Christmas Putz of Central Moravian Church is an elaborate landscaped display that tells the Christmas story through a series of 16 miniature biblical scenes.

(left) Intricately made miniature figures such as this one are featured in the Christmas putzes of Bethlehem.

rocks, driftwood, and evergreens used for the pastoral scene. Following the construction of the set, the intricately made figurines, often family heirlooms of European origin, are positioned in a number of miniscenes depicting the nativity. Each putz is a personal interpretation of the Christmas story and reflects the aesthetic aspirations of the creator.

During Christmas Moravian families go "putzing." That is, they visit fellow Moravians to view their putzes and share the Christmas story. It has been said that in earlier days it was common practice to hang a Moravian star in a window as an invitation to view the putz inside.

Since putzing is largely confined to Moravians, community putzes have been built in Bethlehem for the ecumenical community. These putzes are an elaborate version of the family nativity display—complete with lights, narration, and music. The major biblical events leading to the nativity are spotlighted in chronological order to a seated audience.

The Musical Tradition

Music has been a long-standing tradition within the Moravian church, dating back to the fifteenth century when Jan Hus, a Bohemian priest, was silenced at the stake in 1415 by Roman Catholic authorities for his reformist views. Believing that worshipers should participate more in their services, Hus introduced congregational singing in the native tongue rather than in the customary Latin. His followers, who founded the Unitas Fratrum in 1457, endorsed this anachronistic practice. Today music, both vocal and instrumental, is a vital part of the daily life and worship among Moravians.

The Moravian Music Foundation, founded in 1956 and headquartered in Winston-Salem, North Carolina, is a testament to the role music has played within the Moravian church. The foundation seeks to preserve approximately 10,000 musical documents from the eighteenth and nineteenth centuries, many in manuscript form. Few other churches have archival collections of this magnitude.

This resounding affinity for music is evident in the early history of Bethlehem. Within three years of the settlement of Bethlehem, the Collegium Musicum, a 14-piece orchestra of mostly brass instruments, was formed. They played frequently at town functions and continued the European custom of "tower music."

In 1754, the Trombone Choir took over this responsibility of playing from the tops of buildings on special occasions. Today, the all-trombone ensemble from the Moravian congregation of Bethlehem plays from the belfry of Central Moravian Church. A high note of the Christmas season is when the trombonists herald the arrival of Advent from the belfry the fourth Sunday before Christmas. The group claims to be the oldest continuous musical organization in the country and one of two groups solely devoted to trombones.

Several milestones mark Bethlehem's musical heritage. In 1811, the first American performance of Haydn's oratorio, *The Creation,* was presented at the recently built Central Moravian Church. In 1900, Bach's "Mass in B Minor" was also presented in its entirety for the first time in America at the church during the first Bach Festival.

Although the Moravian church dominated the early days of Bethlehem, the incorporation of the Borough of Bethlehem in 1845 opened the community of approximately 1000 Moravians to outsiders. The Industrial Revolution of the second half of the nineteenth century combined with the establishment of the Bethlehem Steel Corporation at the turn of the century attracted waves of immigrants, mostly European. Also the proximity of Bethlehem to the major urban centers of Philadelphia (55 miles to the south) and New York (85 miles to the east) helped fuel a period of rapid growth, which resulted in today's diverse ethnic community of 71,000 people.

The new immigrants were quick to build their own churches. Today Bethlehem has almost 100 congregations, only six of which are Moravian. Understandably, Bethlehem has been referred to as a "city of churches."

Bethlehem's new cultural traditions have combined with the earlier Moravian heritage to produce a Christ-

The Central Moravian Church belfry and the candlelit windows of Moravian College's Church Street Campus glow during Christmastime in Bethlehem's historic district.

mas schedule that resounds with music. The world-famous Bach choir presents a Christmas concert at the First Presbyterian Church. The Cathedral Choral Society performs Handel's *Messiah* at Lehigh University's Packer Memorial Church. A sing-along performance of the *Messiah* is held at Salem Lutheran Church. A late afternoon organ music series is scheduled daily (except Sunday) in the old Moravian Chapel in the historic area. Morning worship caroling is open to the public on one Sunday during the season at Central Moravian Church and St. Peter's Lutheran Church. Lehigh University, Moravian College, and Moravian Academy present their Christmas vespers. The Moravian churches hold their lovefeasts and candlelight services. Even though these Christmas season events are free, tickets are required.

Another performance that has become a favorite in the last decade is a blend of music and theater in the form of the Live Bethlehem Christmas Pageant. A donkey for Mary and camels for the Magi are among the many animals and the 150 costumed actors in this outdoor reenactment of the nativity. A choir and narrator direct the movements of the volunteer children and adults cast in this one-hour production, usually scheduled just before Christmas.

Architectural Landmarks

The early Moravians, hardened by years of persecution, labored diligently to build a lasting community in the New World. Twenty-one buildings erected in pre-Revolutionary War days are still standing. These original and restored buildings combine with their nineteenth-century counterparts to form Bethlehem's architectural heritage.

In addition to the bus tours, walking tours are offered by several museum and historical preservation organizations. The costumes worn by the volunteer guides are characteristic of the eighteenth-century colonial era. The utilitarian and communal-minded Moravians dressed with simplicity. Men wore the customary breeches, long stockings, shirts, and waistcoats. The women wore a distinctly Moravian outfit—plain ankle-length dresses were

Christmas lights strung on trees and Victorian gas lamps illuminate Bethlehem's historic Main Street. The restored 1758 Sun Inn with its candlelit windows highlights the downtown area.

protected by long aprons, and jackets covered chemises worn as undergarments. For special occasions, such as church, the women wore the *haube*—a white linen cap beaked over the forehead. Both men and women in the early Moravian church were segregated into "choirs" that indicated their marital status and position within the community. The color of ribbon with which the haube was tied indicated to which "choir" a woman belonged. For example, single women wore pink ribbon; married women wore light blue ribbon.

The guides interpret the Old World charm of the massive eighteenth-century stone buildings, which stand as monuments to the Moravians who built a town in the wilderness. Most are built of sandstone and limestone, locally quarried by the pioneers.

The early Moravians relied on the buildings in European Germanic communities as architectural prototypes. As a result the largest collection of original Germanic buildings in America is said to line Church Street. They are not reconstructions, but original structures that have been in continuous use for almost 250 years. The buildings feature symmetrically arranged windows crowned with brick arches, sloping roofs, and dormers.

The cluster of stone structures that line both sides of the street were built to accommodate the homogenous groups of the Moravian communal choir system. They are the Sisters' House (1744), the Bell House (1745), the Brethren's House (1748), and the Widows' House (1767).

The only building not made of stone on West Church Street, the residential center of early Bethlehem, is the oldest remaining building in the city. The *Gemein Haus* was built in 1741 as the "community house" to succeed the small log cabin where the first Christmas Eve service was held. The five-story building, covered with clapboard in 1868, is supposedly the largest log structure still standing in the United States.

The 1751 chapel was built to replace the outgrown "Saal" or worship room in the Gemein Haus. Today, the first place of worship in Bethlehem, the "Saal," is partially preserved as a part of the Moravian Museum in the Gemein Haus. The museum is the oldest of its kind in Bethlehem featuring early Moravian artifacts.

The final worship site for the Moravians built in 1803-1806, Central Moravian Church, was designed with a seating capacity of 1500 for a community less than half that size. It is said to have been the largest church built in Pennsylvania at the time. Today the seating has been

scaled back in favor of a more comfortable atmosphere for 1200 worshipers.

Farther up Main Street, surrounded by downtown businesses, are the Sun Inn and the Goundie House. Fully restored to its original splendor in 1982, the Sun Inn was built in 1758 as the community's first hostelry. Its guest registers have been signed by such notables as John Hancock, Samuel Adams, Benedict Arnold, Ethan Allen, and George and Martha Washington.

The federal-style home of John Sebastian Goundie was built in 1810 and is thought to be the first brick residence in Bethlehem. The interior of the home was recently restored as the final phase of a preservation project by Historic Bethlehem, Inc. Several furnished rooms in the museum shop are open to the public.

Bethlehem's first log cabin in 1741 overlooked the Monocacy Creek, where an industrial complex of some 30 trades and crafts sprung up within a few years. Today the 10-acre eighteenth-century industrial area, administered by Historic Bethlehem Inc., preserves part of this early "industrial park." Several restored buildings are open to the public and tours by costumed guides are available.

The tanning process is demonstrated in the three-story limestone tannery and a large water wheel operates reconstructed mechanisms in the 1762 Waterworks. It is considered to be the first municipal water pumping system in the American colonies. The 1869 brick Luckenbach Grist Mill, site of earlier mills, features interpretive exhibits, offices, and a gallery of contemporary crafts. A replica of a log springhouse is located near the Waterworks.

Not to be forgotten are the Kemerer Museum of Decorative Arts near the center-city complex on Church Street and the Apothecary Museum off Main Street near the Central Moravian Church. The Kemerer Museum, a former mid-nineteenth century residence, offers a glimpse of Bethlehem's gracious past. Two centuries of high-style furnishings and art decorate luxurious rooms and galleries. Bethlehem's original apothecary dates back to 1752 and until 1951 was the oldest drugstore in continuous operation in America. Today the Apothecary Museum contains many medicinal relics and is shown by appointment through the Moravian Museum and Tours.

Bethlehem will celebrate its 250th anniversary from the second half of 1991 until the first half of 1992. A year-long calendar of events is being planned to mark the founding of Bethlehem in 1741. Among these events is an ecumenical candlelight service scheduled just before

Christmas in the 6500-seat Stabler Arena. Yet anniversary officials do not wish to disturb the revered and dignified celebration of Christmas in Bethlehem, the Christmas City, U.S.A. As one spokesperson has said: "December is already a busy enough time in Bethlehem."

One of the largest Moravian stars in Bethlehem hangs above worshipers at Central Moravian Church.

A Quiet Chamber Kept for Thee

WALTER WANGERIN JR.

THIS IS THE WAY it was in the old days:

The milkman still delivered milk to our back door, summer and winter; the milk came in bottles, and the bottles were shaped with a bulge at the top for the cream, you see, which separated after the milk was bottled. Cream was common in those days. So was butter. Margarine was less appealing because, according to Canadian law, it had to be sold in its original color, which was white like lard, and could be colored yellow only by the customer after she had bought it. Or so my mother told me. She mixed an orange powder into the margarine to make it butter-yellow.

But this is the way it was in the old days:

The milkman still drove a horse-drawn wagon, arriving at our house in the middle of the morning. And especially in the winter we would, as my mother said, "tune our ears to hear his coming." That is, we listened for the kindly, congregational clinking of the glass in his wagon as he toiled down our particular street, then we rushed to an upstairs window and watched. In the cold Canadian air, you could hear his coming from far away. We were breathing on the window long before the milkman came bustling up our walk with bottles in a wire basket. And that, of course, was the point: my mother wanted us to bring the milk in right away, or else it would freeze and the cream would lift its hat on an ice-cream column: "How-do-you-do?" "Fine, thank you, Cream, and how are you?"

But this is the way it was especially on Christmas Eve Day: We spent the major portion of the morning at that upstairs window, giggling, whispering, and waiting for the milkman to come. Tradition. My mother was glad to be shed of us on the day she "ran crazy" with preparations. I think we knew that then. But for our own part, we did truly want to see some evidence of how cold it

was outside. It was important that Christmas Eve be cold. And it was the milkman's mare, you see, who presented us with evidence.

So here came the mare in a slow walk, nodding, drawing the wagon behind her even when her master was rushing up sidewalks, making deliveries. She never stopped. And the mare was blowing plumes of steam from her nostrils. Her chin had grown a beard of hoarfrost. Her back was blanketed. The blanket smoked. The air was cold. The air was very cold, and our stomachs contracted with joy within us, and some of us laughed at the rightness of the weather. So here came the mare, treading a hardened snow. The snow banked six feet high on either side of the street, except at sidewalks and driveways; the snow was castles of which we would be kings tomorrow. The snow collected on the mare, whose forelock and eyelashes were white. She shivered the flesh on her flanks, sending off small showers of snow; and so did we shiver. Ah, cold! The air was a crystal bowl of cold! The day was perfectly right.

And we could scarcely stand the excitement.

Downstairs, directly below us in the house, was a room which had been locked two days ago against our entering in. This was my father's tradition, which he never varied year to year. Always, he locked the door by removing its knob, transfiguring thereby the very spirit of the room; all we could do was spy at the knob-hole and wonder at the mysteries concealed inside. My brothers and sisters pestered that hole continually, chirping among themselves like snowbirds on a holly tree, puffing their imaginations like feathers all around them.

Tonight, on Christmas Eve itself, we would all line up, and my father would slip the knob back into the door, and one by one we would enter the wondrous room. This much we knew: the Christmas tree was in there.

23

Therefore, even in the morning at the upstairs window, we could scarcely stand the excitement.

Tonight! And lo, it was very, very cold.

Let me be more specific. We were living in Edmonton, Alberta, then. The year was 1954, and I was ten, the oldest of seven children. I've implied that we were all excited on that particular Christmas Eve morning, and so we were; but though my brothers and sisters could manifest their excitement with unbridled delight, I could not mine. I absolutely refused to acknowledge or signal excitement. They loved the sweet contractions in their stomachs. I was afraid of them. For I had that very year become an adult: silent, solemn, watchful, and infinitely cautious.

So my brothers and sisters laughed and clapped the day away. They spilled colored sugar on cookie dough and covered the kitchen table with a sweet mess, all unworried, unafraid. They claimed, by faster stabs of the finger, their individual treasures from Sears catalogs, and so they allowed their dreams to soar, and so they passed the day. I didn't blame them. They were innocent; they could dare the dangers they didn't see. These children could rush headlong toward the evening recklessly. But I could not.

I held myself in a severe restraint. Because—what if you hope, and it doesn't happen? It's treacherous to hope. The harder you hope, the more vulnerable you become. And what if you believe a thing, but it isn't true? Well, the instant you see the deception, you die a little. And it hurts exactly in your soul, where once you had believed. I knew all this. I had learned that excitement is composed of hope and faith together—but of faith and hope in promises yet unkept—and I was not about to let excitement run away with me, or I would certainly crash as I had crashed the year before.

None of us could stand the season's excitement. But I was frightened by mine and chose to show it to no one.

Last Christmas Eve, in the midst of opening his presents, my brother Paul had burst into tears. I didn't know—and I don't know—why. But I was shocked to discover that the Christmas time was not inviolate. I was horrified that pain could invade the holy ceremony. And I was angry that my father had not protected my brother from tears. There was a fraud here. The traditions were as thin as a crystal globe and empty. I could do nothing about that when I was nine years old, nothing but sob in sympathy with my brother, nothing but grieve to the same degree that I had believed.

But by ten I was an adult; and if Christmas gave me nothing really, and if the traditions could not protect me from assault, then I would protect myself.

No: the more excited I was, the more I was determined not to be, and the more I molded my face into a frown.

I'm speaking with precision now. None of us could stand the season's excitement. But I was frightened by mine and chose to show it to no one, not to my father, not to my mother, and not to myself.

Adult.

By supper the world was black outside, so the noise

inside seemed louder than it had been, and we the closer together. In bathrobes we ate soup. We had bathed: bright faces, soft faces, sparkling eyes in faces glowing with their goodness. Children smile with a self-conscious piety on Christmas Eve, nearly drowning in convictions of their goodness. My brothers and sisters ran to their bedrooms, bubbling, and began to dress themselves.

I stood before the bathroom mirror and combed my hair with water, unsmiling.

Always we went to church on Christmas Eve to participate in the children's service. Nothing happened at home till after that. This was the tradition; and tradition itself began when we would venture into the cold, cold night, on our way to perform the parts we had been practicing for endless Saturdays. And if we were nervous about the lines we had to say, well, that only intensified excitement for the time thereafter, the room, the mystery, and the tree.

My hair froze as soon as I walked outside. It crackled when I touched it. It felt like a cap. Cold. My face tightened in the night wind, and I blew ghosts of steam which the wind took from my lips. They were leaving me and wouldn't come back again.

The family sat three, three, and three in the three seats of a VW van, I in the farthest corner of the back, slouched, my hands stuffed in my pockets. I forced myself to repeat my lines for the pageant. I was to be Isaiah.

So then it was a blazing church we crowded into, a small church filled with yellow light and stifling excitement. People were laughing simply at the sight of one another, as though familiar faces were a fine hilarity; "You, Harold, ha-ha-ha, you! Well, Merry Christmas to you!" In the narthex the press of people squashed us because we wore thick coats; and the children were shooed downstairs to giddy into costumes, and the adults clumped upstairs to wait in pews, and holly greens were knocked from the windowsills, and the windows were black with night. Who is so foolish as to laugh in such an atmosphere and not to fear that he's losing control? Not me.

Class by class the children trooped into the chancel. As the pageant proceeded they sang with wide-open mouths all full of faith, eyes unafraid. The little ones waved to their parents by the crooking of four fingers,

like scratching air. They positively shined with happiness. No one thought to be fearful.

I, in my turn, stared solemnly at the massed congregation and intoned, "For unto us a child is born, unto us a son." I saw the adults jammed shoulder to shoulder in ranks before me, nodding, craning, encouraging me by grins, not a whit afraid. "Wonderful, Counselor—" No one was ready to cry in the midst of so much cheer and danger. Naive people—or else they were cunning. Well, neither would I. "Mighty God!" I roared. I would not cry. Neither would I succumb to the grins of these parents, no. "Everlasting Father!" Oh, no, I would not risk disappointment again this year. "The Prince of Peace!" I thundered, and I quit. No emotion whatsoever. I did not laugh. I did not smile. Both of these are treacherous. I made a glowering prophet altogether. My father and mother sat nearly hidden ten rows back. I noticed them just before descending from the chancel.

Walnuts, tangerines, a curled rock candy all in a small brown bag—and every kid got a bag at the end of the service. A bag was thrust toward me, and I took it, but I didn't giggle and I didn't open it. *No, sir! You won't entice me to gladness or gratitude.*

And the people, humping into coats again, called, "Merry Christmas! Merry Christmas!"—the pleasant tumult of departure. They were flowing outward into the black night, tossing goodwill over their shoulders: "Merry Christmas!" *No, ma'am! You won't disarm me again this year.*

Even now my father delayed our going home. Tradition. As long as I can remember, my father found ways to while the time, increasing excitement until his children fairly panted piety and almost swooned in their protracted goodness.

"Don't breathe through your noses," my father sang out, hunched at the wheel of the van. This was his traditional joke. "You'll steam the windows. Breathe through your ears," he called.

Silliness. We breathed through our noses anyway, frosting the windows a quarter-inch thick, enclosing our family in a cave of space in the night. With mittened hands and elbows we rubbed peepholes through the muzzy ice. We were driving through the city to view its Christmas decorations, lights and trees and stables and

beasts and effigies of the holy family. This, too, was tradition.

I looked out my little hole and regarded the scenes with melancholy.

There was a tremendous tableau of Dickensian carolers in someone's yard, some dozen people in tall hats and scarves and muffs, their mouths wide open, their eyes screwed up to heaven in a transport of song, their bodies a wooden fiction. They didn't move. They didn't produce a note of music. So nobody heard them. But nobody minded. Because no one was singing. And no living body was anywhere near them anyway.

This was worse than silliness. This was dangerous. I found myself suddenly full of pity for the wooden figures, as though they could be lonely in the deserted snow. Any feeling at all made me vulnerable. I stopped looking.

My boots crunched snow when we walked to the door of our house. A wind with crystals caused my eyes to tear. But resolutely, I was not crying.

And still my father delayed our going into the room.

Oh, who could control the spasms of his excitement? Oh, Dad! Let's *do* it and be done with it!

We lined up in the kitchen from the youngest to the oldest. I stood last in a line of seven.

But it was tradition, upon returning home, that we change our church clothes into pajamas and gather in the kitchen.

Across the hall the door was still closed—but its knob had been replaced. I saw that knob, and my heart kicked inside of me. So I chewed my bottom lip and frowned like thunder: *No! It won't be what it ought to be. It never is.*

Adult.

And always, always the hoops of my father's tradition: we lined up in the kitchen from the youngest to the oldest. I stood last in a line of seven. My littlest sister was clasping her hands and raising her shining, saintly face to my father, who stood before her facing us. Her hair hung down her back to the waist. Blithe child! Her blue eyes burst with trust. I pitied her.

My father prayed a prayer, tormenting me. For the prayer evoked the very images I was refusing: infant Jesus, gift of God, love come down from heaven—all of the things that conspired to make me glad at Christmas. My poor heart bucked and disputed that prayer. No! I would not hope. No! I would not permit excitement. No! No! I would not be set up for a second disappointment.

We were a single minute from entering the room.

And I might have succeeded at severity—except that then we sang a song, the same song we had always sung, and the singing undid me altogether. Music destroys me. A hymn will reduce me to infancy.

Nine bare voices, unaccompanied in the kitchen, we sang: *Ah, dearest Jesus, holy child*—and I began to tremble.—*Make thee a bed, soft, undefiled*—The very sweetness of the melody caused my defenses to fall: I began to hope, and I began to fear, both at once. I began to wish, and wishing made me terrified. I began all over again to believe; but I had never ceased my unbelief. I

25

began to panic.—*Within my heart: that it may be*— Dreadfully, now, I yearned for some good thing to be found in that room, but "dreadfully," I say, because I was an adult; I'd put away the childish things; I'd been disillusioned and knew no good to be in there. This was a pitiless sham!

—*A quiet chamber kept for thee.*

My father whispered. "Now."

He turned to the door.

Little squeals escaped my sister.

He grasped the knob and opened the door upon a muted, colored light: and one by one his children crept through the door and into that room.

All of his children save one. I lingered in the doorway, looking, not breathing.

There, shedding a dim and varied light, was the Christmas tree my father had decorated alone, every single strand of tinsel hanging straight down of its own slim weight since he hung them individually, patiently, and would not hasten the duty by tossing them in fistfuls (tradition!)—the tree he had hidden three days ago behind a knobless door.

But there, unaccountably, was my father, standing center in the room and gazing straight at me.

There, in various places about the room, were seven piles of gifts, a pile for each of us.

There, in the midst of them, my mother sat smiling on the floor, her skirts encircling her, her own radiance smiting my eyes, for she verged on laughter. My mother always laughed when she gave presents, however long the day had been before, however crazy she had almost gone. I began to blink rapidly.

But there, unaccountably, was my father, standing center in the room and gazing straight at me. At me. And this is the wonder fixed in my memory: that the man himself was filled with a yearning, painful expectation; but that he, like me, was withholding still his own excitement—on account of *me*.

Everything else in this room was just as it had been the year before, and the year before that. But this was new. This thing I had never seen before: that my father, too, had passed his day in the hope that risks a violent hurt. My father, too, had had to trust the promises against their disappointments. So said his steady eyes on me. But among the promises to which my father had committed his soul, his hope, and his faith, the most important one was this: that his eldest son should soften and be glad.

If I had grown adult in 1954, then lo, how like a child my father had become! The colored lights painted the side of his face. He gazed at me, waiting, waiting for me, waiting for his Christmas to be received by his son and returned to him again.

And I began to cry. O my father!

Silently, merely spilling the tears and staring straight back at him, defenseless because there was no need for defenses, I cried—glad and unashamed. Because, what was this room, for so long locked, which I was entering? Why, it was my own heart. And why had I been afraid?

Because I thought I'd find it empty, a hard, unfeeling thing.

But there, in the room, was my father.

And there, in my father, was the love that had furnished this room, preparing it for us no differently than he had last year prepared it, yet trusting and yearning, desiring our joy.

And what else could such a love be but my Jesus drawing near?

Look, then, what I have found in my father's room, in my heart after all: the dearest Lord Jesus, holy child— the nativity of our Lord.

I leaned my cheek against the doorjamb and grinned like a grown-up ten-year-old and sobbed as if I were two. And my father moved from the middle of the room and walked toward me, still empty-handed; but he spread his hands and gathered me to himself. And I put my arms around his harder body. And so we, both of us, were full.

This is the way that it was in the olden days.

The Tree of Jesse

From Medieval Times to the Present

PHILLIP GUGEL

URING THE TWELFTH century in Europe the Tree of Jesse became a popular subject for artists. Many medieval and renaissance examples of the Jesse Tree in various media still exist in a complete or partial state. There are Jesse Trees embossed on leather book covers, embroidered on altar hangings and vestments, painted on parchment, plaster, wood panels, or canvas, pieced with mosaic, engraved as prints, sculpted in metal or wood, and assembled from stained glass.

Though its popularity declined during the 1600s, some artists have continued to reinterpret the Tree of Jesse's fascinating imagery. It remains a key illustration for Advent and Christmas art and deserves to become better known. The six examples discussed and illustrated here enrich our celebration of God's coming among us, and can serve to deepen our appreciation of some of the often appealing and imaginative ways artists illustrated this biblical subject.

The biblical basis for the Jesse Tree's imagery comes from Isaiah 11:1-2: "There shall come forth a Rod from the stem of Jesse, And a Branch shall grow out of his roots. The Spirit of the Lord shall rest upon Him, The Spirit of wisdom and understanding, The Spirit of counsel and might, The Spirit of knowledge and of the fear of the Lord." This is the only prophecy from the Bible that has inspired art on a continuing basis, according to Emile Mâle, the noted French art historian. The record of Jesus' ancestors found in the first chapter of Matthew's gos-

pel and in the third chapter of Luke's gospel are the chief New Testament sources used to determine who is featured in the family tree.

The Tree of Jesse visually interprets the prophet Isaiah's words concerning the Messiah's lineage. It

fig. 1.

links Jesse, the father of King David (progenitor of the royal dynasty that gave the Old Testament nation of Israel its golden age of monarchy), with Jesus the Christ or Messiah. Its simplest form shows Jesse lying asleep as a stem, tree trunk, or vine rises

from his loins. Jesus appears at the top of the tree or vine with the Holy Spirit. In some versions the Virgin Mary is present, with or without Jesus, and certain Old Testament kings and prophets, such as David and Isaiah, are shown.

Eventually the Tree of Jesse's design grew in complexity as additional Old Testament kings and prophets, nonbiblical figures, and narrative scenes from both testaments were incorporated. The versions picturing Jesus' family tree or genealogy developed from artists' reinterpretations of Matthew and Luke's differing accounts of Jesus' lineage. What makes these later Jesse trees interesting, in many instances, are the liberties artists took as they chose the subjects for their visual record of Jesus' ancestry.

In addition to interpreting his family tree, the Jesse Tree shows how artists illustrated the relationship between the Old and New Testaments by using typological parallels. *Typology* concerns the relationship between Old Testament events, persons, and themes that prefigure parallel New Testament ones. This method of interpreting the Bible, which is central for Christianity, explains the Old Testament in light of the New Testament. In one Jesse Tree window from the fourteenth century in Germany, for example, the Old Testament story of God's revelation to Abraham and Sarah that she will bear a son is shown in a narrative scene parallel to another illustrating the New Testament story of the annunciation, when the angel Gabriel tells the Vir-

fig. 2.

figure, this representation is very unusual, if not unique, among early renditions for its depiction of Jesse as dead and lying in a coffin. No one has offered a convincing explanation for this peculiar and puzzling detail, nor is any given in the *Siegburg Lectionary.*

A very stylized tree grows through the coffin and culminates in a flower with seven shoots, which in turn end in seven medallions. Each medallion encloses a dove, symbolizing one of the gifts of the Spirit mentioned in Isaiah's prophecy. These are identified by the script around each medallion.

Except for its ornamental frame, the illumination is simple and lacks much detail. The medallions overwhelm its flat two-dimensional space.

Another illumination (fig. 2), this one from the *Ingeburg Psalter,* copies the classic form of Jesse Tree imagery that evolved in France during the twelfth century. Its design, which dates from about 1210, was influenced by the Jesse window (c. 1145) found at the Abbey Church of Saint Denis near Paris. The abbey's window served as a prototype for the designers of the Jesse windows at Chartres and York Cathedrals, as well as for many manuscript illuminators.

As a possible allusion to his importance, Jesse is drawn larger than the other figures. His bedcovers show v-folds, a stylistic characteristic that helps to date illuminations painted during this era.

The tree looks more like a plant or vine; its colorfully painted, stylized tendrils partially enclose the two kings and the Virgin Mary above Jesse. The kings add a whimsical touch to the piece as they offer a serenade on harp and viol. The tree completely encloses Jesus at the top and forms a sort of *mandorla* (an oval around an entire figure indicating divinity or holiness). Seven doves symbolize the Spirit's gifts for the Messiah.

At the tree's left in descending order are an angel and the Old Testament prophets Malachi, Daniel, and Amos. The latter hold scrolls, their identifying attribute, with quotations in Latin written upon them. The dove hovering near each prophet symbolizes that their words are divinely inspired.

gin Mary that she will give birth to the Messiah. As the new Adam and descendant of Jesse, Jesus becomes the prime example of a typological approach and the fulfillment of Old Testament prophecies. This particular window illustrates many such parallels.

Other tree imagery from the Bible, which became part of the repertoire of subjects used in Jesse Tree designs, include the tree of knowledge of good and evil, Moses' burning bush, Aaron's flowering rod, Jesus as a vine, and the tree of the cross on which Jesus died.

The earliest Jesse Tree image featured here is an illumination from a manuscript known as the *Siegburg Lectionary* (fig. 1), which was painted for a church in Cologne, Germany, during the early twelfth century. (An illumination is a drawing or picture done with tempera colors on parchment or vellum. A manuscript is a book whose script is written by hand. A lectionary is a book containing the appointed texts from the Bible for the church year, which are read at mass).

Belonging to a category of Jesse Trees in which Jesse is the dominant

To the tree's right in descending order are another angel, a sibyl, the prophet Ezekiel, and the patriarch Joseph. (In Greek and Roman mythology, sibyls were women thought to have powers of divination and prophecy. They often appear in Christian art because it was believed they foretold Jesus' coming.)

The gold background and stylized architectural frame enhance the clear symmetrical design, refined figures, ornamentation, and pleasing colors of this wonderfully appealing illumination.

The identity of the painter of the third *Tree of Jesse* shown (fig. 3) has been a matter for debate among Northern Renaissance art historians. The majority of them, however, attribute this panel to Jan Mostaert (c. 1472-1554?) who served as dean of the painters' guild in the Dutch city of Haarlem on three different occasions.

Mostaert's version exhibits an exaggerated realism in sharp contrast to the two medieval examples with their stylized, two-dimensional imagery. Its realism imparts a worldly rather than spiritual character to the Jesse Tree. Full of complex imagery and religious allusion, its dense composition is at once intriguing and overwhelming.

Holding a book open to his prophecy that inspired the Jesse Tree's imagery, Isaiah, another prophet, and a nun kneel in meditation around Jesse. The nun is a new subject here. Her position indicates she is the painting's donor, though we do not know her name. Including a donor's figure in a work of art was not unusual. The Abbot Suger appears in the Saint Denis Jesse Tree.

David and eleven other kings of Judah perch in the tree, spread out in an amusing array of poses. Will their weight break its branches? Their elegant clothing—the ermine collars and boldly striped hose, for instance—not only gives them a dandified appearance, but visually pro-

fig. 3.

29

fig. 4.

claims their exalted status in Old Testament history.

Enthroned at the top of the tree and surrounded by adoring angels as she holds the Christ child, the Virgin Mary becomes the painting's dominant figure. (Her glorification as the rod or shoot from Jesse's root who becomes Jesus' mother is apparent in the imagery of many medieval Jesse Trees, as well as in the stanza of a hymn by Fulbert of Chartres).

Mostaert's arcane visual references to Mary honor her for other roles besides that as the bearer of God's Son. Influenced by popular cults in the church devoted to this piety and teaching, and by the wishes of his patron, perhaps, he painted a peacock (symbolic of her role as Queen of Heaven), an enclosed cloister garden (symbolic of her immaculate conception and purity), a bandolier of red and white roses worn over the shoulder of the king above Isaiah, and several rosaries (symbolic of the rosary as a popular devotion to Mary).

Probably painted between 1504 and 1505, Mostaert's *Tree of Jesse* is the most convincing realistic rendition of this subject in Europe to that time. Though its tree is frontally placed as in the medieval versions,

the artist gave it a sense of spatial recession by making the higher figures in the tree smaller than the lower ones, and by placing the tree within an enclosed garden setting. Unfortunately, the painting's compositional and spatial clarity are obscured by its many figures. The attention to detail and use of color, however, are masterful.

Unlike Mostaert, Jean Tassel (1608-67) was not concerned with complex details of iconography in his painting of *The Tree of Jesse* (fig. 4). This serenely joyous version also honors the Virgin Mary as the Messiah's bearer. The 12 kings of Judah are here too, as her court of honor. In this canvas, however, the tree and its occupants are massed against a dramatic landscape.

Tassel spent at least 13 years studying and working in Italy. He became influenced by the painter Caravaggio from Naples, whose compositions display dramatic contrasts of darkness and light. His Jesse Tree exhibits a similar stylistic approach. Jesse's large figure, for example, reclines in semidarkness with only his hands and turban highlighted. The Virgin and Christ child, however, appear in full light. A halo of light, containing the heads of cherubs, surrounds

them and illumines the central portion of the horizon as well.

Jean Tassel's Jesse Tree is a charming example of his style. Compared to Mostaert's version, its composition seems clearly defined; the figures are not crowded and his imagery does not overwhelm the viewer. The 12 kings are animated in their facial expressions, gestures, and postures, giving them a sense of individuality. Mary's dominant figure takes on Michelangelesque proportions. Tassel's use of subdued color imparts a dusky richness to his canvas and to the convincingly rendered textures of the figures' lavishly ornamented robes.

The son of a noted provincial painter, Jean Tassel spent the remainder of his career working in the region of his birthplace in northeastern France, where he decorated churches and did small genre, history, and portrait paintings.

The Tree of Jesse significantly declined in popularity with baroque, rococo, and neoclassical artists. During the nineteenth century, however, there was a revival of interest in medieval art in England and France, particularly in that from the Gothic era. As a result, many church buildings from that era were restored.

One such restoration began in 1859 at Waltham Abbey, Essex, England. The next year the director of its restoration commissioned Edward Burne-Jones (1833-98) to design a Jesse Tree for the church's east window over the altar. Easily the most spectacular example shown here, it spreads across three "lights" or separate windows (fig. 5).

Fabricated by James Powell of the Whitefriar's Glass Company, its iconography reveals some unusual aspects. Each window relates a group of Old Testament figures to Jesus' nativity.

In the central window Jesse is shown surrounded by the symbolic figures of the four evangelists. Each holds a streamer on which appear the opening words of each of their gospels. To Jesse's left are the eagle for John and the angel for Matthew. To his right are the ox for Luke and a wonderfully regal lion for Mark. Eight Old Testament kings populate the tree branches above: Achaz, Solomon, David, Roboam, Hezekiah, Manasseh, Josias, and Jeconiah.

The three roundels in the central window's upper section depict the crucifixion, nativity, and shepherd's visit. They revive subjects found in medieval Jesse Trees. According to Martin Harrison, it seems possible that Burne-Jones knew of the crucifixion scene in the Jesse window at Wells Cathedral and imitated it in his design. It provides a fitting climax to the window's imagery and places Jesus' birth in its proper perspective. The central window is wider than the two side windows to accommodate its design.

The left window portrays Old Testament judges and patriarchs. In descending order they are Moses, Samson, Joshua, Gideon, Jacob, Noah, plus Adam and Eve. Of this number, only Adam, Jacob, and Noah are mentioned by Luke and Matthew in their genealogies, so this window presents more than a literal depiction of some of Jesus' ancestors.

The right window depicts Old Testament prophets. Isaiah appears at the bottom and above him Jeremiah, Ezekiel, Daniel, Habbakuk, and Malachi. John the Baptist, Jesus' forerunner and key New Testament prophet, is at the top.

All figures in this intricate composition are connected and unified by the Jesse Tree's multiple twining branches spreading through the three lancets (pointed windows). The skillfully done representations of the figures with their animated bodies, varied poses, and expressive faces look just as vigorous today as when they were first created. The artist's love of pattern is evident in the figures' costumes. Further unity in his design is achieved by the blue tonalities of the glass used for the background. The first-rate fabrication of the glass used in these windows produces glowing, jewel-like colors with captivating visual effects. The boldness and rich scale of colors evident in Burne-Jones' Jesse window led Sir Nikolaus Pevsner, eminent English art historian, to judge it as one of the best stained-glass windows done in the nineteenth century.

Sir Edward Burne-Jones received more than 67 commissions for stained-glass window designs during his career. He grew up in Birmingham and attended Oxford University, where he met William Morris. The lure of becoming an artist led him to give up his plans of becoming

fig. 5.

a priest. In London he studied with Dante Gabriel Rossetti, a leader of the Pre-Raphaelite painters in England. This group, which Burne-Jones and Morris joined, advocated a return to the careful craftsmanship and serious intent found in the art of the late medieval and renaissance masters.

The *Tree of Jesse* (fig. 6) in the west transept of Pilgrim Lutheran Church, Saint Paul, Minnesota, presents us with an imaginative example of adapting this subject's traditional imagery for the present time.

Its figures are situated in three vertical registers, the more important ones placed in the wider central register. Its pointed top complements the lancet windows of the Gothic revival church building it adorns. Two sinuous vines, one on each side of the center, climb upward to form Jesse's tree.

A unique aspect of this Jesse Tree is its inclusion of the wives of the men shown as Jesus' ancestors. At the base of the central panel are Jesse and his wife (unnamed), followed by David and Bathsheba, Solomon and Naamah, Zerubbabel and his wife (unnamed), and finally the figure of the boy Jesus in the Temple. The inscription above him reads "my Father's house," a reference to the story in Luke about his visit to the Temple in Jerusalem. Picturing Jesus as a boy here is unusual.

Jesus' precursors pictured on the left register in ascending order are Abraham and Sarah, Isaac and Rebekah, Jehoshaphat and his wife (unnamed), and Josiah and Zibidah. The unicorn above them is a symbolic reference to Mary's virgin birth. At the top stands Mary herself, waving a branch as she searches for her son.

Members of Jesus' family tree pictured on the right register in ascending order are Jacob and Rachel, Ruth and Boaz, Judah and Tamar, and Hezekiah and Hephzibah. The 14-pointed star above them symbolizes the arrangement of Jesus' an-

cestors into three groups of 14 generations each as recorded by Matthew in his genealogy. At the top is Joseph, with his hand to his mouth as if he is calling for the boy Jesus, a further allusion to Luke's story of the Temple visit. In all, 26 of the 90 ancestors of Jesus listed in the Bible appear in this example's inconography.

The *Tree of Jesse* at Pilgrim Lu-

fig. 6.

theran Church was planned by the parish's current pastor, the Rev. Paul Schuessler. It was sculpted in low relief on oak by Arthur Stolp, a parish member, and his assistant, Richard Miller, in 1982. Originating as a memorial for two parish members, the Jesse Tree panel is inscribed with their names along with Isaiah's Jesse prophecy. The expressionistic, simplified style of this Jesse Tree offers a fresh alternative to the refined style of some of the earlier examples.

The designs of these six Jesse Trees represent a span of 800 years. One reason they remain perpetually interesting is that each exhibits some artistic license taken by its creator to imaginatively, rather than literally, interpret this biblical subject. You might say that the artist "winked" in planning and executing each design. Showing Jesse in a coffin, the mythological figure of a sibyl, or the donor, are all departures from the biblical record, as are the emphasis on Mary, the inclusion of ancestors born before Jesse's time, and the depiction of the wives of some of Jesus' forebears. Yet all of these imaginative departures in each version add to their visual power and may deliver their own message. The inclusion of the wives of those Old Testament men in the Pilgrim Lutheran Church Jesse Tree, for example, gives timely recognition to these women, who were also Jesus' ancestors, instead of ignoring their role as links in his lineage.

In the history of the Jesse Tree, five different types of design have emerged. These types are identifiable in the examples shown. The Siegburg illumination features Jesse as the key subject, one type of Jesse Tree. The Ingeburg illumination illustrates the "classic type" of Jesse Tree. The paintings by Mostaert and Tassel emphasize the Virgin Mary through her placement in the tree, size, and use of symbolic imagery. Though it also shows nativity narrative scenes, the superb Jesse Tree by Burne-Jones depicts the crucifixion as a key portion of its design, reviving a type of late medieval Jesse Tree. The unusual subjects of the Pilgrim Lutheran Church version put it in a "special type" category. All of these types are of interest and value as part of the Jesse Tree's long history of imaginative design, whether fanciful or sober.

The Tree of Jesse reminds us of Jesus' Old Testament roots, of his coming that we celebrate during Advent and Christmas, and of his gifts to us which no one else can bring.

CHRISTMAS TREES REMEMBERED

BY BOB ARTLEY

ARTLEY '89

It is, no doubt, the fragrance of the freshly cut evergreen tree more than anything else that evokes memories of Christmas for me. My first experience with that fragrance, although I would have been too young to remember it, was when I was six months old. It is hard to say what impression that first tree might have made on my young mind. Yet, from my earliest years the Christmas tree was certainly a part of my accumulated impressions, which have built up since then into a rich store of Christmas memories.

One of the very first Christmas trees I remember came from a tall spruce in our front yard that Dad had already decided would be cut down as the yard was so dense and shaded with evergreens grass would not grow under them. So it was decided that the spruce's removal would begin by cutting off its top for our Christmas tree.

A day or two before Christmas, while Mom and I watched from an upstairs bedroom window, Dad climbed to the top of the tall spruce near our front porch. He secured a rope around the portion that was to be our Christmas tree, then sawed it off and gently lowered it to the snowy yard below.

It all seemed a part of the Christmas magic, when that little tree, which only moments before had been living up somewhere near heaven, stood green and fresh in our living room, waiting to be adorned. The boughs were wet from melted snow and were cold and prickly to the touch. The magic fragrance of fresh evergreen that is so much a part of Christmas flooded the room.

ARTLEY '89

Once we had exhausted the supply of fresh trees from our front yard, we made our selection from the bedraggled collection of little trees that leaned against the outside wall of the local grocery store.

Selecting the right tree was not easy. But it was remarkable how, from that forlorn stock of compressed and misshapen tree specimens, there could be chosen one that when set up and decorated and put in a place of honor in the home would be transformed into a thing of beauty and meaning — our family Christmas tree.

I can still see my parents making the selection. Dad would reach in among the branches of one of the trees, grasp it around its trunk and raise it up and bring it down sharply, thumping its sawed butt against the frozen ground or cement sidewalk. If this "shock test" didn't jolt its needles loose it was a likely candidate to stand in our living room for a few days to help us celebrate Christmas.

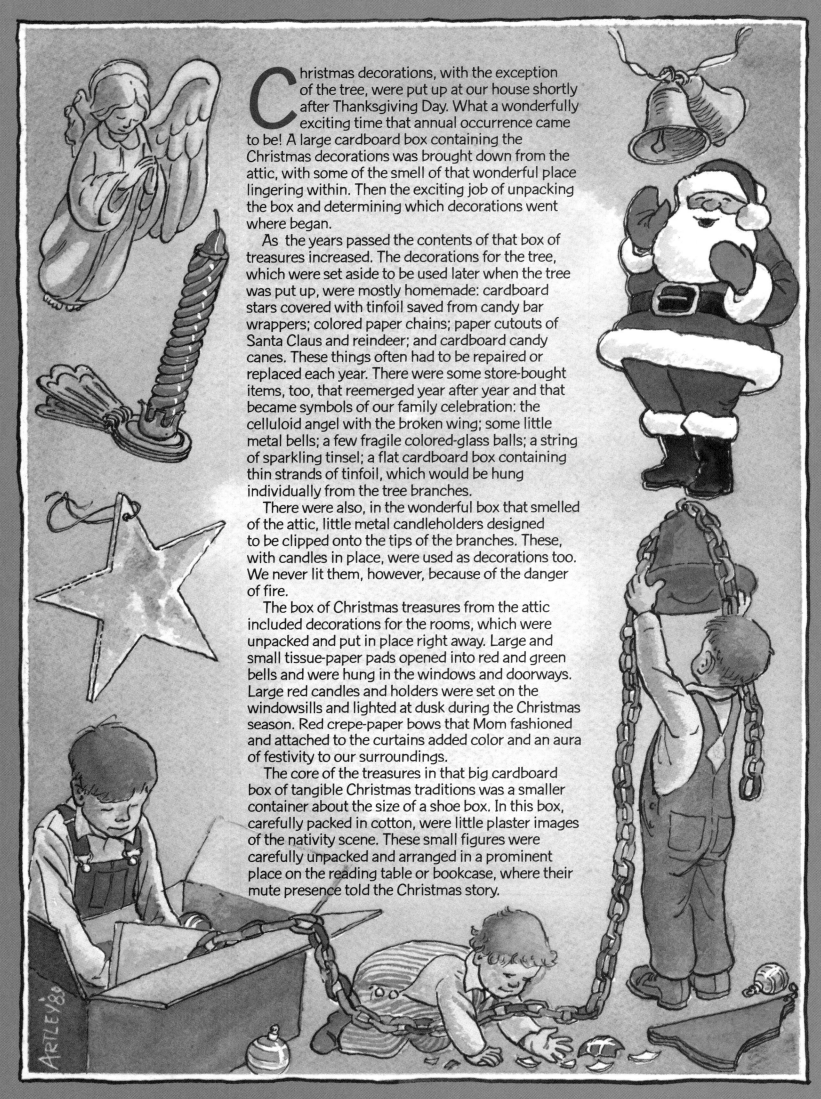

Christmas decorations, with the exception of the tree, were put up at our house shortly after Thanksgiving Day. What a wonderfully exciting time that annual occurrence came to be! A large cardboard box containing the Christmas decorations was brought down from the attic, with some of the smell of that wonderful place lingering within. Then the exciting job of unpacking the box and determining which decorations went where began.

As the years passed the contents of that box of treasures increased. The decorations for the tree, which were set aside to be used later when the tree was put up, were mostly homemade: cardboard stars covered with tinfoil saved from candy bar wrappers; colored paper chains; paper cutouts of Santa Claus and reindeer; and cardboard candy canes. These things often had to be repaired or replaced each year. There were some store-bought items, too, that reemerged year after year and that became symbols of our family celebration: the celluloid angel with the broken wing; some little metal bells; a few fragile colored-glass balls; a string of sparkling tinsel; a flat cardboard box containing thin strands of tinfoil, which would be hung individually from the tree branches.

There were also, in the wonderful box that smelled of the attic, little metal candleholders designed to be clipped onto the tips of the branches. These, with candles in place, were used as decorations too. We never lit them, however, because of the danger of fire.

The box of Christmas treasures from the attic included decorations for the rooms, which were unpacked and put in place right away. Large and small tissue-paper pads opened into red and green bells and were hung in the windows and doorways. Large red candles and holders were set on the windowsills and lighted at dusk during the Christmas season. Red crepe-paper bows that Mom fashioned and attached to the curtains added color and an aura of festivity to our surroundings.

The core of the treasures in that big cardboard box of tangible Christmas traditions was a smaller container about the size of a shoe box. In this box, carefully packed in cotton, were little plaster images of the nativity scene. These small figures were carefully unpacked and arranged in a prominent place on the reading table or bookcase, where their mute presence told the Christmas story.

Our family Christmas tree, which sat in front of the west window of our farmhouse living room, was usually put up and lovingly decorated for the great celebration only a day or two before Christmas. This short period of display not only assured the physical freshness of the tree but also the freshness of its presence in the room as well. If its needles held, the tree was kept up until New Year's Day. Then it was taken out to stand in a snowbank and its branches were garnished with bread crusts for the winter birds.

The tree, which typically was rather spindly by today's standards, was set with its cut end embedded in a pail of wet sand. This helped maintain its freshness a little while longer. But if the tree was to be a part of our celebration for only two or three days, a wooden crosspiece was nailed into the squared-off butt of the tree and served as a base.

In the days before electricity on the farm we could not use colored tree lights. But our Christmas tree, with its tinsel and its foil-covered stars reflecting the warm light of the kerosene lamps in the room, shone and sparkled much like the way the moon and other cold heavenly bodies reflect the light of the sun. I thought it was every bit as beautiful a Christmas tree as those adorned with electric lights.

When my two brothers and I were young we enjoyed several celebrations around a tree each Christmas season. First there was the one at our country school. The teacher provided the tree and all the students had a hand in decorating it.

Then there was an enormous tree at the Christmas Eve service at the church. This tree was beautifully decorated and glowed with electric lights. Following the church service the family returned to Grandma Artley's and gathered around the tree in her living room. This tree, much like the one at our church, was of picture-book quality. Grandma had bought it from the local tree nursery and it was symmetrical, full, and beautifully decorated with colored electric lights, pretty glass balls, and tinsel rope that sparkled and glowed in an otherwise darkened room. It spoke of elegance and beauty and of Grandma's love for her family.

And, of course, the pile of attractively wrapped packages around its base served to enhance the tree's beauty and interest to us kids.

On Christmas Day we completed our round of holiday celebrations by going to Grandma and Grandpa Crow's farm to join with aunts and uncles and cousins on Mom's side of the family.

The tree there looked to be closely related to the one in our living room. There were no electric lights and its decorations were also mostly homemade — chains made from colored construction paper and cones made from wallpaper scraps. These cones hanging from the branches were filled with popcorn and hard candy. Strings of popcorn and popcorn balls wrapped in wax paper added to the simple beauty of the tree.

If one looked with a critical eye one would see a Christmas tree that was neither symmetrical nor well-formed. In fact, it was not a tree at all, but rather a branch cut from a Scotch pine, which was tied and trussed into a more or less unified whole and then propped into the corner of the room. There, in spite of its imperfections, it became the center of our merry gathering of fun and goodwill.

Beneath this misshapen, lovingly decorated tree was spread a white bedsheet. On it were piled brightly wrapped, simple gifts, something for everyone. Many of them, like the decorations, were homemade. Yet this tree spoke as much of the spirit of Christmas and family love and fun as did the well-shaped, exquisitely decorated and lighted tree at Grandma Artley's the night before.

So, whether or not the tree was "perfect" didn't matter to those gathered around it, as long as it was a fresh evergreen with the special fragrance that meant Christmas.

Island Cathedral

JANE MARIE LAZOR

All
activities
vibrated
with anticipation
as the one-room
school was garlanded
with glittery
holiday decorations
unearthed from the dust
in its attic.
It yielded also such treasures
as a fine velvet curtain
for the temporary stage,
antique ornaments for the balsam that
reached the high metal ceiling,
and six giant kerosene lanterns
whose soft light
would envelop the evening performance
of the Christmas program.
A few children took the mission
of gathering boughs for a large wreath.
We set out with migratory determination across
the plowland covered with wind-hammered snow,
magical sculptures that mimicked rolling waves.
Our destination, a black spruce grove,
waited for us in the distance,
a dark island in the endless white expanse.
In the bitter cold a squeaking crunch accompanied
each footstep on the brittle snow.
Finally, the spires of the conifers loomed before us,
piercing the white, sunless sky.
Leaving our saws, we threaded through the
heavy apron of outer branches
and discovered inside a sheltered hollow.
In dim light, we saw the tall, rough trunks of the inner trees were bare,
but their vigorous tops crowned the cavern with a dark ceiling.
We explored the pillared haven with open eyes and hearts,
breathing the incense of pine scent.
Footprints of pheasants and field mice patterned the
light dusting of snow on the deep carpet of needles and cones.
The whistling wind was muffled to a harmony of hushed whispering.
The pilgrimage ended with the grating of our saws,
and laden with branches and cones, we left the spruce grove.
Trudging back over the solidified waves, we ascertained with glee
that the small schoolhouse in the distance was our pirate ship.

Favorite American Carols

MARIANNE SLATTERY

O Little Town of Bethlehem

Phillips Brooks, dubbed "prince among preachers," loved the children of his congregation and wrote hymns especially for them. During the Christmas season of 1868, Brooks devotedly wrote a poem based on his trip to the holy land three years earlier. He had sat in the same fields where shepherds watched their flocks so many years before. The stars' brilliance and the silence of the fields must have made him wonder what it was like for the shepherds to whom the angels appeared. The serenity of these unforgettable memories passed in front of him as his mind flooded with words for his poem.

Carrying his finished poem to the church organist and Sunday school superintendent, Lewis Redner, Brooks asked him to compose music to accompany the words. For weeks no melody would flow. Then one night, a few days before Christmas, the melody came to Redner as he slept. Quickly he awoke and jotted down the notes, then went back to bed. He polished up the composition the following morning in time for the children to learn and sing the carol that Christmas.

It Came upon the Midnight Clear

In 1849, sitting by a fire that December, Edmund Sears composed the words to "It Came upon the Midnight Clear." In it he begs people to stop fighting, to be still "and hear the angels sing." But did anyone listen? Fifteen years later our nation was embroiled in civil war.

As a Unitarian minister and advocate of peace and the abolishment of slavery, Sears is credited with the first Christmas song of social significance, a message that would remain American.

Born in Sandisfield, Massachusetts, on April 6, 1810, Sears later attended Union College at Schenectady, New York, then went on to Cambridge Divinity School. A literary career interested Sears for many years, but from early childhood his deep religious convictions influenced his choice of a vocation in Christian ministry. He ministered in the old Massachusetts towns of Lancaster, Weston, and Wayland.

His vocation as clergyman did allow Sears time for his literary interests. He died quietly in the small community of his parishioners on January 16, 1876, leaving behind many songs, poems, and articles. The favorite and most remembered is the poem he originally titled "That Glorious Song of Old."

Go Tell It on the Mountain

The Negro spiritual was born during the slave era and is characterized by its forceful outflowing of religious passion. Approximately 6000 spirituals exist today, which have been handed down from generation to generation.

The majority of texts for the spirituals come from the Old Testament, especially those passages that speak of the Hebrews in bondage, as they relate most closely to the slave experience. Likewise, some spirituals draw from the New Testament passages that record Jesus' suffering and death. But very few relate the story of Jesus' birth. One that does is "Go Tell It on the Mountain."

Because Negro spirituals were created in the fields or crude cabins of the slaves and passed along as oral tradition, it is impossible to trace the originator of this powerful song. The traditional stanzas of the carol read:

When I was seeker   *He made me a watchman*
I sought both night and day,   *Upon a city wall,*
I asked the Lord to help me,   *And if I am a Christian,*
And he showed me the way.   *I am the least of all.*

Those featured here, however, were written by John Wesley Work Jr., who wrote the three stanzas that relate more to Christmas.

The son of a church choir director, John Work was born August 6, 1871, in Nashville, Tennessee. He majored in history and Latin at Nashville's Fisk University then he became an instructor of Greek and Latin there.

Throughout his tenure at Fisk University, Work led the effort to preserve, study, and perform the Negro spiritual. Fisk himself was the descendant of an ex-slave.

Christmas Bells

Just before Christmas in 1863, Henry Wadsworth Longfellow received news that his oldest son, Charles, a lieutenant in the Army of the Potomac, was shot through both shoulders during the last battle on the Rapidan River in Virginia. A sad father sat in the silence of his home when Christmas bells coaxed him from pensive thought and created the inspiration for a poem.

"Christmas Bells" originally contained seven stanzas. Two stanzas refer specifically to the Civil War and are usually omitted from the carol. Also, so that the song might end with joy, Longfellow's third stanza was moved to the end. Longfellow, however, never intended for his poem to become a song, much less a popular Christmas carol.

GO TELL IT ON THE MOUNTAIN

John W. Work, Jr., 1871~1925, sts. 1, 2, 3
Traditional African American Spiritual, refrain

African American Spiritual
arr. R. Nathaniel Dett

mf **solo**

1. While shep-herds kept their watch-ing o'er si~lent flocks by night,
2. The shep-herds feared and trem-bled, when lo! a~bove the earth,
3. Down in a low~ly man-ger the hum-ble Christ was born,

be~hold through-out the hea~vens there shone a ho~ly
rang out the an~gel cho~rus that hailed the Sav~ior's
and God sent us sal~va~tion that bless~ed Christ~mas

All voices   **Refrain**

light.
birth.
morn.

Go tell it on the moun~tain,

o~ver the hills and ev~ry~where;

go tell it on the moun~tain, that Je~sus Christ is a~born.

American Cloth Dolls

AUDREY FREEMAN TEEPLE

IN HUNDREDS OF households across the land the weeks before Christmas bring a flurry of excitement as preparations for the holidays get under way. Along with the cleaning, the baking, the shopping, and the decorating there is also the creating of a special gift, made in secret, for one very special person. One such special gift that a delighted child will find under the tree on Christmas morning will be a handsewn cloth doll.

For more than a hundred years, grandmothers, mothers, and doting aunts have created some of the most interesting cloth dolls to be found and have established the cloth doll as a part of American history.

The women of colonial times were adept at needlework as testified by the samplers, quilts, and tapestries that have survived from that period. The children of that time would have played more with homemade dolls than they would have played with the expensive wooden dolls imported from Europe. A few examples have remained from that time period, and it is interesting to note that the dolls are rather small in size. Because fabric was so precious, dolls were made of small pieces of material painstakingly sewn together to form body and clothes.

As the settlers moved westward the cloth doll did too, giving comfort to their small owners throughout the arduous trek across prairies, mountains, and plains. These early one-of-a-kind dolls are today collected as primitives and are hard to date, but certain clues do help to place them in an approximate time frame. Methods of sewing and fabrics used are good indications of age. Some of the fabrics used most often from 1850 to 1900 were unbleached muslin, muslin, wool, twill, and stockinette (a soft close-ribbed cotton fabric used for stockings and underwear). The dolls were stuffed with whatever was available—sawdust, crushed nut shells, rags, bran, straw, cotton batting, and even dried beans. The faces were either embroidered or painted on with sepia ink, charcoal, housepaint, or artist oils. Some had wigs of human or animal hair, thread or yarn, or else were just painted. Bodies were made in all shapes and sizes, usually out of proportion. The hands and feet varied from one extreme to the other, either well-defined or just stumps. The clothing, whether simple frock or fancy dress, reflected the time they were made. But no matter how they looked or what they wore the dolls were well-loved. Today they charm us with their quaintness and their air of mystery.

Izannah Walker

The doll created by Izannah Walker of Central Falls, Rhode Island, is said to be the first patented rag doll in the United States. The patent is dated November 4, 1873, but according to relatives Izannah was making her dolls as early as 1855.

The early dates assigned to the creation of her dolls is logical, for the final process that she patented in

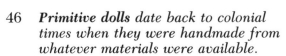

46 *Primitive dolls date back to colonial times when they were handmade from whatever materials were available.*

1873 is complicated in design. There must have been many examples of trial and error before she was satisfied with her creation. The head consisted of a firm inner core of a shaped head and face, over which a padding of cotton was laid. Then came a layer of stockinette. These delightful dolls are made entirely of cloth with the head and limbs painted in oil. The majority of Izannah's dolls had two sausage curls in front of each applied ear and curls around the back of the head. The hair was usually center parted. The dolls have hand-stitched fingers; some models have hand-stitched toes, while others have shoes painted on.

It is said that Izannah dressed each doll herself; her favorite style seems to have been an off-the-shoulder dress, which was the fashion for little girls of the 1860s. How her dolls were marketed is not known. She no doubt started making them as gifts for relatives and friends, was encouraged by their acceptance, took out a patent, and entered the world of commerce.

Julia Beecher

To help raise money for the missionary fund for the Park Congregational Church of Elmira, New York, Julia Beecher created the Missionary Rag Baby in 1885. The doll continued to be made until 1905. Constructed of either pink or black stockinette (old silk jersey underwear was used) the dolls ranged in size from 16 to 23 inches. The face was formed by expert needle sculpturing, then the features were painted in oil. Modeling of the hands varied; some had out-stretched fingers, others a clenched fist. The toes were stitched and the legs were stitched across at the knees so they could bend. The black doll that Mrs. Beecher designed was constructed differently. Only the head was made of stockinette. The body was brown sateen with mitt type hands. This doll also was stitched at the knees.

(above) The dolls in this group were designed by Martha Chase, who wanted her dolls to resemble real children as much as possible. The doll's clothing is fashioned after the clothing of children in the late nineteenth century, when the dolls were made.

(below) The Missionary Rag Baby was created by Julia Beecher to help raise money for a church missionary fund. The dolls were produced from 1885 to 1905. They are rare today, and it is obvious from this doll's well-worn face that it was a well-loved toy.

The wig was knotted brown yarn. The nose and cheeks were molded, the lips embroidered in red, and the eyes were shoe buttons mounted on a white shell-like base. Beecher dolls are rare as not many survived the loving given them.

Martha Chase

In 1889 Martha Jenks Chase of Pawtucket, Rhode Island, began making her dolls. She wanted to make a doll as much like a real child as possible, a doll that a child could love and care for and yet could outlast the not-so-tender care given it. Her children loved the dolls she made so much that Martha soon found herself making them for friends, relatives, and neighbors. In 1891, on a trip to Boston, she went to the Jordon Marsh department store to buy a pair of shoes for a doll that she was bringing to a little girl in Maine. Jordan

Marsh commissioned her to make a number of dolls to be sold through their retail store. What had begun as a hobby developed into a full-scale business.

A tiny wooden building was constructed behind the Chase house at 22 Park Place in Pawtucket. Although this was the center for the business, it was primarily a cottage industry as the women who were employees worked on making the doll parts at home. The assembly, painting, and shipping was done from the Doll House, as the building was called.

The early dolls were made of molded stockinette with sateen bodies and were stitched at the hips, knees, and elbows so they could bend. The Chase printed label can be found either under the left arm or on the upper part of the left leg. The clothing for the Chase dolls was fashioned after children's clothes of the time. Boy dolls wore rompers; girl dolls wore dresses that featured smocking and tucks.

Then around 1911 Martha began work on an adult-size mannequin that could be used for hospital training purposes. The principal of the Hartford Hospital Training School for Nurses wrote Mrs. Chase and asked if she could make an adult-sized doll that could be used as a training model for nursing students. Martha Chase, with the help of her husband, tackled this new project. They made patterns, worked out methods of construction, and developed an adult figure that stood 5'4" in height. This hospital training doll was produced for over 50 years.

The Philadelphia Baby

Made around the turn of the century, not much is known about this mysterious rag doll except that it was made for the J. B. Sheppard Co. department store of Philadelphia, Pennsylvania. It is a well-made doll with a lot of attention given to the facial features. Unfortunately the painting on the face is very thin with no protective coating and the dolls are usually found in poor condition with many facial cracks. The head and neck were constructed of a fairly coarse grade of stockinette material. To attach the head the base of the neck was hand sewn to the muslin body with an overcast stitch. The features are quite rugged with prominent cheeks that give the dolls a boyish look. They are not stitched at the elbow so the arms do not bend, but they are stitched at the hip and knee. There is no evidence that they had any printed trademark or pasted label. Mysterious as she is, she is a welcome addition to any doll collection.

The Lithographed Doll

A truly American invention, the lithographed doll was produced by many American companies. Sold in sheets to be cut out and stuffed by the home sewer, these dolls are hard to identify for the mark of the company was cut away when the doll was assembled.

On December 20, 1886, Edward S. Peck of Brooklyn, New York, obtained a patent for a cloth St. Nicholas doll. Cut out, sewn, and stuffed, it made a special Christmas toy. Animals were also designed as cloth toys. The first of these was Tabby Cat, printed on a half yard of cotton material by Arnold Print Works.

The company, which was located in North Adams, Massachusetts, manufactured printed fabrics by the yard. Following the success of Tabby they quickly produced other animals and dolls. In 1894 they advertised Palmer Cox Brownies, Little Tabbies, Tatters, Little Tatters, Bunny, Monkey, Owl, Hen and Chickens, Soldier Boys, and Little Red Riding Hood.

Art Fabric Mills of New York from 1899 to 1910 also made such printed cloth dolls as Buster Brown and Punch and Judy. Their merchandise line also included boy, girl, baby, and black dolls, plus some animals.

The popularity of these printed rag babies attracted the attention of doll manufacturers like E. I. Horsman of New York and Albert Bruckner of New Jersey. Each produced a series of ready-made dolls that had attractive printed faces. The trade name for the Horsman dolls was Babyland Rag and although their faces were appealing they were just the flat cut-and-sew variety. Bruckner on the other hand gave his dolls stiff mask faces with modeled dimples, cheeks, and eyes. His dolls are signed on the shoulder with the patent date of 1901. Black dolls as well as white ones were made by both firms and both produced a topsy-turvy doll as well. A topsy-turvy doll is one that has two heads, one on either end. The skirt hides one head while the other head is in view. One head is a white doll with blond hair usually wearing a blue dress while the other head is a black doll with black hair and a red dress.

Ida Gutsell of Kirkville, New York, was a teacher of painting and modeling who applied for a patent for a printed doll in 1893. Her doll was manufactured by the Cocheco Manufacturing Company. This doll design differed from other printed dolls of the period. Instead of being a flat two-dimensional doll, her design was three-dimensional in part. There was a seam down the center of the head, front and back, to round out the head in a natural manner. The design also included clothing, consisting of a blouse, a jacket, and trousers. Complete instructions for making the doll and clothing were printed on the material along with a small printed picture of the finished doll.

The printed doll has also been used as an advertising premium. In the early 1900s, companies such as

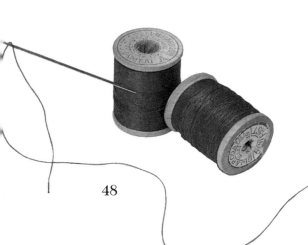

Ceresota Flour and the Cream of Wheat Company used cloth dolls as a popular way to advertise their products. Some of today's companies still use the cloth doll as an advertising premium. Who isn't familiar with the dolls made to represent the Jolly Green Giant, Lil Sprout, Burger King, the Campbell Soup Kids, and the Eskimo Pie Boy?

The topsy-turvy doll, a type of lithographed doll, was produced by doll manufacturers in the early twentieth century. The doll is made with two heads— the doll's skirt hides one head while the other is in view.

Other Cloth Dolls

Perhaps the most famous of all American cloth dolls are Raggedy Ann and Andy. In 1914 when Marcella Gruelle was 12 years old she found an old faceless rag doll in the attic. It had belonged to her grandmother. She showed it to her father, artist Johnny Gruelle, and asked him to draw a face on it. The famous shoe button eyes, red triangle nose, and irrepressible grin of Raggedy Ann was born. Marcella, inspired by the poem "Raggedy Man" written by James Whitcomb Reilly, called her doll Raggedy Ann. The doll became Marcella's constant companion. When Marcella died at age 14, her father in his grief and in her memory began writing the Raggedy Ann stories. To promote the books the original doll was displayed with them in the bookstore window. Customers were so intrigued by the doll that they wanted to purchase her and orders began pouring in. The Gruelle family made the dolls for about a year and then awarded the patent rights to the Vollard Company, who in turn

added Raggedy Andy to the production line. They also introduced some of the other characters found in the stories—Beloved Belindy, Uncle Clem, Johnny Mouse, Percy Policeman, Cleety the Clown, Sunny Bunny, and Brown Bear.

Through the years different companies took over the patent rights and the Vollard characters were dropped except for Beloved Belindy. The Knickerbocker Company continued to produce Raggedy Ann and introduced the Camel with the Wrinkled Knees. Georgene Novelties marketed Raggedy Ann and Andy and also Beloved Belindy from 1938 to 1963. The dolls have a cloth label sewn in the side seam of the body. A perennial favorite, Raggedy Ann and Andy have been made since 1915 and are still being made today.

Most everyone is familiar with the dolls of Madame Alexander but are not aware that the very first dolls made by the Alexander Doll Company were of cloth. Some of the first dolls made were of a Red Cross nurse and a baby. Fascinated by characters

from literature, Madame Alexander created dolls from such classics as *Alice in Wonderland, Little Women,* and from the novels of Charles Dickens. In 1938 Susie Q and Bobby Q were marketed. These all-cloth dolls have red or yellow yarn hair, a mask type face, a tiny closed mouth, button nose, and with their striped stockings wear white felt spats.

The earliest dolls were done by Madame Alexander or one of her three sisters. They are all beautifully painted. As the company grew, the intricate hand painting had to give way to automation and the work was done by machine. Some of the characteristics of the early dolls were lost but the quality of the dolls was never sacrificed.

Another famous doll artist, Grace G. Drayton, creator of Dolly Dingle, also designed cloth dolls. Two companies, the Bently-Franklin Company and the Colonial Toy Manufacturing Company, produced her dolls. Many of her dolls bear the copyright symbol and her signature. These dolls were advertised as the "Hug-Me-Tight" dolls and were sold as flat sheets along with embroidery floss for the features, to be sewn and stuffed at home. The Dolly Dingle series of cloth dolls was manufactured by the Averill Manufacturing Company of New York from 1922 to about 1932. Her copyright and signature appear on the tags.

Doll Artists of Today

Carrying on the time-honored traditions of the early cloth doll makers are three talented young women from three different parts of the United States—Jane Cather of California, Jan Farley of Iowa, and Judie Tasch of Texas. Each of these doll makers has contributed her special abilities and imagination to the wonderful world of dolls.

Lithographed dolls have been produced by many American companies since the late nineteenth century. They were sold in sheets to be cut out and stuffed by the home sewer.

Jane Cather

In 1981 Jane Cather of Carmel Valley, California, formed her company, "Made by Night." The only time she had available for making dolls was late at night and this name, mysterious and magical, seemed just right for her new business. Jane had an established career in art and design before she turned to making original cloth dolls and animals. Her whimsical characters are garbed in exquisite clothing that makes use of lovely fabrics both new and antique. Fine details and accessories are likely to include old jewelry, buttons, ribbons, and laces. Each doll is one-of-a-kind. The dolls have a soft, natural look and appear to have led very interesting lives. Her patterns for each doll design are hand-made and she weaves a special story about each one of her dolls.

Jan Farley

Because of her mother's interest in doll collecting, Jan Farley began the study of antique dolls at the early age of 16. In the collection was an Izannah Walker rag doll that held a special place in Jan's affections. When she decided to create rag dolls of her own design, the primitive beauty of these early folk art dolls served as her inspiration.

This doll, created by Jane Cather of California, is one-of-a-kind, as are all of Cather's delightful doll creations. A popular modern doll artist, Cather creates a special and unique story to accompany each of her dolls.

Raggedy Ann and Andy are among the most familiar and well-loved of all American cloth dolls. They have been made since 1915 and are still being made today.

Stitching a personality into each of her dolls, Jan found herself creating caricatures of people she had known since childhood. Each doll is hand-sculptured. Their heads, bodies, hands, and feet are made of rag. They are painted and treated to take on a lifelike quality. Since they are hand-crafted, no two dolls are alike. The clothes are designed from old fabrics and they often wear antique jewelry. The approximate size runs from 25 to 27 inches. Just as Izannah Walker's dolls are folk-art treasures, Jan Farley of Blue Grass, Iowa, designs her Country Folk Dolls not to create a business but to create a legacy.

Judie Tasch

Each doll that Judie Tasch of Austin, Texas, fashions from fabric, paste, and paint is christened with a name that reflects its personality. The first cloth doll she designed bears the name Serenity Wisdom. Other dolls soon followed and they also bear whimsical names. Adam Pittsfield is Serenity's beau. Then there is Constance, Harley, Lulu Belle, and Cordelia, just to name a few.

In 1950 Judie began making dolls to sell so she could share her creations with others. Influenced by the early doll makers such as Izannah Walker and Martha Chase, her original designs are inspired by these antiques. The dolls are made of cotton and painted in several stages, antiqued with a glaze and then varnished. Each is named and is signed and dated. Their vintage clothing is made of old fabric when it is available. Deftly stitched and wonderfully painted, each doll pays tribute to the skills of the early doll makers. They recreate the charm of the past and capture the hearts of today.

(top) Jan Farley's modern creations are inspired by the primitive beauty of early folk-art dolls. Each doll is handcrafted and no two are alike. Many of Farley's dolls are caricatures of people she has known.

(bottom) Judie Tasch began making dolls in 1950. Tasch gives each of her dolls a name that reflects its personality, and each doll is signed and dated.

The study of cloth dolls is a fascinating adventure into history. The ingenuity and resourcefulness of the early doll makers is marvelous to behold and it is fortunate that so many examples of these fragile creatures have survived these many years. The original dolls of today's artisans will someday have their place in history too, for they are as painstakingly made as the early dolls, have as much character, and are cherished by their modern-day owners as were the dolls of yesteryear.

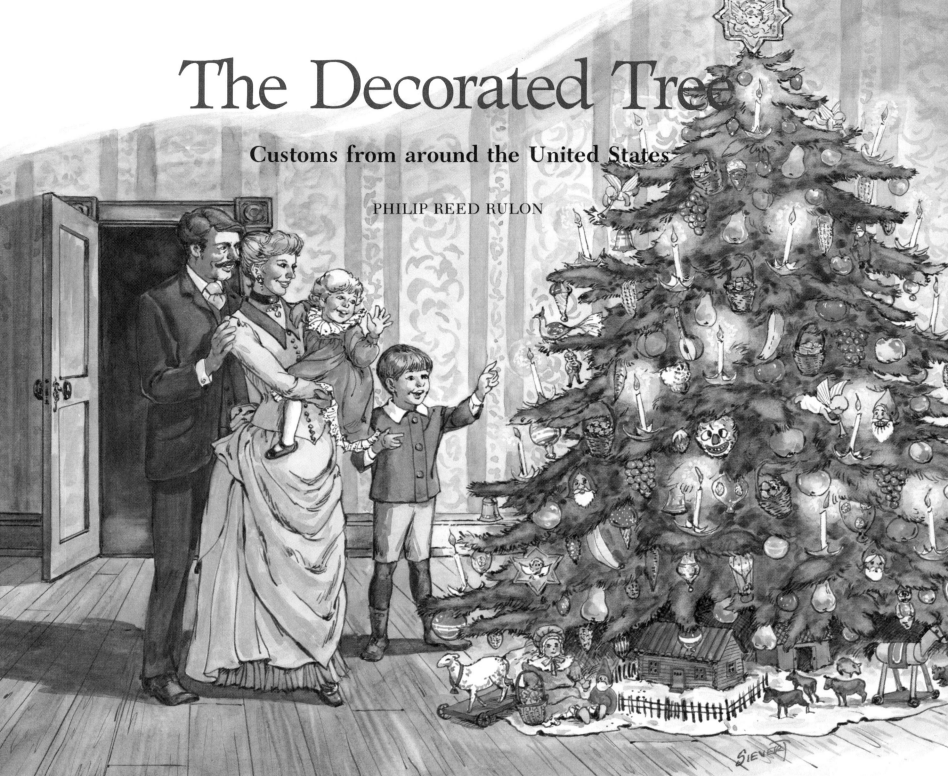

The Decorated Tree

Customs from around the United States

PHILIP REED RULON

MANY NATIONS HAVE contributed to the celebration of Christmas in the United States. The Italians institutionalized the holiday and developed the concept of the Madonna and Child. French musicians transformed the carol into an art. The followers of Odin in Scandinavia came up with the idea of a Yule log. The English instituted the use of holly, ivy, bay, rosemary, and laurel as holiday decor, as well as the familiar dinner, complete with mince and fowl. One of the most charming contributions, however, came from Germany—the ever-popular Christmas tree.

It is believed that farmers from the Rhine provinces of Germany brought the tree to Pennsylvania in the westward migration that occurred after America obtained its independence. From there, it moved quickly to New York and New England, and followed the frontier to the Great Lakes and the Middle West. Other factors account for establishing the Christmas tree in the antebellum South and both cavaliers and Yankees took the tree to the Great American West after the Civil War.

German

The earliest American tree decorations followed the standard in Germany of placing a star or angel at the top. The remainder of the fir or hemlock would wear home-spun necklaces of gilded walnuts or popcorn and many-colored glass balls. Special figurines made of glass were produced in Germany by cottage industry crafters for sale, often becoming heirlooms. The latter included artificial icicles, with replicas of regional fruits or animals imbedded inside. In German-American communities, the tree would be decorated in secret by the adults of the household. On Christmas Eve the parlor doors would be opened and the children would be afforded their first view of the darkened room adorned with a candlelit tree. Sometimes a child on his or her "first Christmas" would receive a brightly lit miniature tree all of his or her own.

Christmas became a major export of Germany. Large manufacturing companies developed to make ornaments for consumption at home and abroad. In the 1870s, a glassblower at Lauscha (in the forests of the Thuringian Mountains) named Louis Greiner-Schlottfeger, created

51

a thin fragile ball called *kügeln* by blowing glass into a wooden cookie mold. Later, he added a silvering solution that produced a mirrorlike shine. Some writers estimate that 5,000 different kinds of shapes were produced from 1870 to 1930. In 1890, F. W. Woolworth, the department store magnate, purchased 200,000 ornaments from the glassblowers of Lauscha to sell in his five-and-dime stores located throughout the United States. In 1899, Woolworth holiday sales reached a half-million dollars and he began paying his workers a Christmas bonus to insure a loyal labor supply.

The Dresden, a detailed three-dimensional figure, is another innovation. The ornament, an animal, boat, fish, or bird, was made from two pieces of gilded or silvered cardboard (usually two halves) that were pressed together. As the designs became more complex, such as a masted ship, the pieces were parceled out to cottage industries to assemble. Often these workers added innovations, such as a sail for a ship, a silk skirt for a ballet dancer, or drawstrings for a candy bag. The ensuing delicate works of art were often hung from a feather tree. These trees, made from splitting goose and turkey feathers in half and wiring them onto a simulated trunk lodged in a turnstand, provided an elegant background for the precious decorations. World War II interrupted the manufacture and export of such items on a permanent basis, because many of the most famous factories were bombed in 1945. Later, for a community behind the Iron Curtain, the manufacture of Christmas ornaments did not have a high priority.

Pennsylvania Dutch

American immigrants improvised on decorations for their Christmas trees. The Pennsylvania Dutch inhabitants of Lancaster and Carlisle counties, for example, did not have the funds to purchase kugels and Dresdens from the homeland. Thus, angels and stars for the top of the tree were often hand-carved, while cookies and cakes made from almond paste, sugar, and egg whites were decorated with cameo images modeled after more expensive designs. The latter, called *matzebaum*, were baked, then were painted with dyes made from berries and vegetables. A variation, named *springerle*, contained images created from pressing egg dough seasoned with anise into carved wood or tin molds prior to baking.

Swiss-Germans in this region favored *tirggel* for ornamental cookies. These edible pastries, a delightful blend of honey, flour, and sugar, were paper thin and almost transparent. The final product, complete with painted design, would usually be hung in front of a candle on the tree, so that the light behind could create a shimmering shadow of color. The *tragout*, an inedible cousin made from mixing tragacanth gum and dough together, could be molded like clay into objects like birds, flowers, trumpets, and even manger images. Besides cookie ornaments, Pennsylvania Dutch families made garlands of almonds, raisins, popcorn, and *schnitz* (dried apples) to hang on the tree branches. Sugarplums, dyed walnut or egg shells, and homemade stuffed animals provided the final touches unless one of the family wanted to frost the tree with a mixture of water, flour, and sugar.

Scandinavian

Immigrants from Sweden, Norway, and Denmark brought different traditions to the American Middle West. The principal decoration for them was a *Julbuk*. This is a facsimile of a billy goat constructed from wrapping straw around a cardboard tube and attaching this with wire to woven-straw sheaves resembling a head and legs. At one time or another, Catholics and Protestants alike banned the *Julbuk*, believing its origins could be traced to a pagan ceremony called *Joulu* that celebrated the return of the sun each December. But, as is often the case in other cultures, public popularity, in this case for the goat, eventually superseded dogma and reason.

Swedes often begin the Christmas season with an Advent tree, which is carved from wood. Each day of the week before Christmas children place a miniature bird on the branches. When there are no more birds to affix, the family knows that the festival is at hand. The Christmas tree, however, may be strewn with brightly wrapped caramel candy, as well as paper angels, mittens, doves, reindeer, bird houses, flags, and, perhaps, ship pennants. Dolls made of yarn complete the decorations, except for saffron-flavored buns called Lucy Cats. The latter are named for Saint Lucia, an early Swedish martyr who legend suggests appeared in a white robe beneath a crown of light to feed starving peasants.

Norwegians, like Swedes, use straw in decorating for the holidays. In addition to *Julbuks*, a straw crown is woven and suspended from the ceiling above the tree. To the crown are added straw diamonds that dance in midair when the slightest breeze causes them to stir. The top of the Christmas tree itself is reserved for three candles, which represent the Magi, while the lower branches hide people and animals important in the nation's harvest. Colorful paper ornaments contrast with the green of the tree and the golden straw saved for Christmas from the summer fields.

The Danes, the last of the Scandinavian triad, celebrate Christmas with an intensity that inspired a native son, Hans Christian Anderson, to write many tales of the season. The most peculiar innovation for the tree are caricatures of gnomes, elf-like leprechauns called *Julnisse* who are thought to live in the lofts and cellars of Danish homes. These little men are dressed in farmer's homespun, with white clogs and red stockings and hats. Their presence is much desired, for they love children and cats and bring good luck to the households in which they reside. Adults are fond of placing miniature flags of their country and region on their trees, while children prefer glazed paper heart-shaped baskets loaded with candy, crackers, and gingerbread people in addition to trinkets made of tinsel and bright-colored paper.

English

While the Great Lakes region deserves recognition for the most variations, the honor for the most intense celebration of Christmas belongs to the Atlantic Seaboard states directly below the Mason-Dixon Line. In 1608, the new governor of Virginia, John Smith, set the standard for the Anglican South when he said: "Wherever an Englishman may be, and in whatever part of the world, he must keep Christmas with feasting and merriment." From Christmas Eve to Twelfth Night, Southerners gathered on the plantations for parties, foxhunts, and dances at which both European and indigenous foods and wines were served in good taste with great abundance.

The English in America, both North and South, began to incorporate Christmas trees into their holiday celebrations because of an event that occurred in England in 1841. Prince Albert, who had been born in Coburg (a small town in south-central Germany) put up a tree in Windsor Castle in December for his twelve-month-old son, Albert Edward. This tree may have been the most delectable one in history, so says one scholar, as trays and baskets bearing the most expensive sweets that could be bought hung from its limbs. Cakes and gingerbread were suspended by ribbons, with other delicacies laid under the branches on a white damask covered table. French candies, in the shape of cottages, knights, soldiers, and dolls completed the culinary delight. All of these items rested under a winged angel on whose outstretched hands were suspended colorful wreaths. Prince Albert's popularity with the masses in England motivated the working classes to decorate a facsimile of Albert's tree. Writers, such as Charles Dickens, who saw the tree in person, disseminated the idea of a decorated tree throughout the Empire and America through their stories of the Victorian Age.

Frontier

In 1862, the passage of the Homestead Act by the national legislature facilitated settlement of the Mid-, South, and Northwest sections of the United States. The pioneers who farmed the land, or those who migrated to raise cattle or work in copper, gold, and silver mines, brought the concept of Christmas along with them to the frontier west of the Mississippi. Compared, however, to those of Europe or the Eastern Seaboard, celebrations were crude. In places such as Franklin County, Iowa, the inhabitants had to go some 20 miles to the Iowa River just to find an evergreen. Subsequently, a community tree was placed in the courthouse and representatives of the various churches came on a staggered schedule to hang their homespun decorations of apples, candles, and popcorn garlands on it.

On the Texas prairie, where trees were also scarce, a substitute for green trees often had to be found. In Van Horn, one family tied together three tumbleweeds in a triangular shape. Popped corn was strung on white thread and raw, red cranberries were strung on strands of red cotton for color. A homemade star, cut from paper and framed with wire, completed the trimmings. In Arizona, the last of the original 48 states to enter the union, makeshift decorations for rural families were the rule, not the exception, until as late as the 1920s. And, as in other parts of the United States, it was often German-Americans who carried the culture of the Christmas tree beyond the pale. During the Civil War, a man in Prescott by the name of Rodenburg led an expedition to locate and then decorate a tree in a miner's shack. A Black man from New Orleans made three different kinds of blackjack candy which others wrapped in manila paper dusted with flour to hang on the tree. Large tallow candles from wagon boxes were tied to tree branches with rawhide strips for

lights. Women searched their trunks for bits of jewelry and/or snips of ribbon to hang on the limbs. Finally, rag dolls were sewn from worn-out clothing to hang on the limbs, and animals, boats, little carts, and soldiers were whittled from wood by men handy with jackknives to add a finishing touch.

Farther North, at Inscription House, an isolated trading post located on the Navajo Reservation near the Arizona-Utah border, Native Americans and Anglos came together in the post-World War I era to decorate a piñon tree that had been cut from the slopes of the San Francisco Peaks. The community decorated its tree with small bells and colored-glass globes, as well as with the traditional strings of popcorn, cranberries, and piñon nuts. Imitation icicles and strips of tinsel were carefully placed on the various branches. (These items had been ordered from mail-order catalogs.)

Over the tree, on the ceiling, hung a red, paper bell (accordian type) and from it were strung streamers that went to all parts of the room. The Indians liked to receive food and drink, such as fresh fruit and Arbuckle coffee, as gifts while the trading families relished the concho belts, turquoise squash blossoms, and silver bracelets made by tribal craftspeople, that had been tied to the branches of the tree. Gradually, as modernization came to the West, homespun decorations were replaced by inexpensive imitations of precious items used elsewhere.

The Christmas tree and its adornments, which originated in the Rhine provinces of Germany, has become an esteemed part of our American heritage, permeating household celebrations in all parts of the nation. The manner in which individuals and institutions decorate may differ, reflecting a particular cultural or religious heritage, but the concept of a decorated tree as part of the national celebration is universal.

The General Grant

Our National Christmas Tree

JERRY D. LEWIS

IT MIGHT BE CALLED the "evergreening of America." Each year, some 50,000,000 Christmas trees decorate the country's homes and businesses. One tree, however, stands apart. No string of multicolored lights dangles from its branches. Its only decoration is a pristine mantle of fresh snow. Nevertheless, it lifts the spirits of the thousands who journey to see it the second Sunday of each December.

To tell the story of that tree, we must go back to 1924, to Sanger, California. Many doing their Christmas shopping one bright, sunny December afternoon waved as Charles E. Lee's horse and carriage rode by. From Sanger, Lee headed toward the nearby Sierra foothills. He rode up into a light snow until he reached the edge of the Grant Grove of giant sequoias.

One of the big trees, the General Grant, had been spreading its roots for some 4000 years before that December afternoon. The giant redwoods have survived from an ancient lineage of huge trees that sprouted over much of the earth many centuries ago. Today, for reasons not entirely understood, the giant redwoods have disappeared, except for scattered groves on the western slope of the Sierra Nevada range.

Threading his way through the sequoias, Lee at long last approached the General Grant. He stopped and stared in awe. The tree soars 267 feet into the sky, the height of a 26-story building. It stands that tall despite the fact that its upper part was destroyed centuries ago, perhaps by lightning. Before that catastrophe, it probably stood close to 400 feet. Grant's lowest branch hovers 130 feet above the forest floor, and the circumference of its virtually fireproof trunk measures 107 feet.

The General Grant ranks as one of the oldest living things on earth. It had already stood in the forest primeval for more than 2000 years on that blessed night when a birth in Bethlehem changed the history of the world.

To Charles E. Lee, the General Grant must have looked especially beautiful that afternoon, frosted with the season's first snowfall. He stared in almost shocked

silence until he was startled by a tiny hand grabbing his. Looking down he saw a small child, her eyes open almost as wide as her mouth. She exclaimed, "What a wonderful Christmas tree that would be!" Then, turning, she ran off into the grove, probably to rejoin her parents.

Lee never learned her name, but he couldn't forget her words. The following year, he recruited some friends and local business people. Together, they trekked over what was then a snow-covered, pothole-gutted narrow dirt road to the park. Reaching the tree, Lee placed a bunch of wildflowers beside it, then held a short, informal service under the broad limbs.

His elation following the service moved him to write a long, impassioned letter to the White House. Government was smaller and more accessible in those days. Within four months, on April 28, 1926, President Calvin Coolidge accepted Lee's suggestion and designated the General Grant as the nation's Christmas tree.

During December that first year of the tree's official status, a group of about 200 people gathered at Sanger to make the trip. This time they brought along not only a pastor, but also a choir and a wreath. After the floral decoration was laid at the base of the tree, an interdenominational service was held. In addition, holiday messages were read from both President Coolidge and Major U. S. Grant III, grandson of the Civil War general.

Over the years, the annual program, which is held every year on the second Sunday in December, has been expanded. Visitors still enjoy scriptural readings, but the ceremonies now also include the singing of carols led by local choirs, plus an address by a noted speaker.

Anyone who wishes may join the thousands who come from every state to participate in the holiday festivity at Kings Canyon National Park. Those who can't attend the ceremony this season, or even the next, need not worry, however. The nation's Christmas tree has been growing in the same fertile soil for some forty centuries, so it's likely to be waiting in all its magnificence whenever one gets around to paying it a visit.

Growing a Holiday Tradition

Christmas Tree Farming from Seed to Sales Lot

MARVIN THRASHER

LAUGHINGLY, excitedly, the first customers of the season come to a cut-it-yourself Christmas tree farm.

This is the day for which the trees were planted. The dozen or more years of seed gathering, seedling planting, shaping, and spraying of the growing trees have come to an end. The joy of seeing all the happy faces makes the long wait of the tree farmer worthwhile. The joy of seeing the tree topped with an angel or a star makes the long, cold winter weeks until a new planting season begins quite bearable. But, let's start at the beginning of the tree-growing story.

Seed Collecting

From cones gathered in autumn at Colorado blue spruce groves that have been certified as free of disease by state foresters, the winged seeds of the blue spruce are collected by both full-time professionals and part-time amateurs. As many as 8000 cones may be required to fill a bushel basket, but often one mature tree will yield two and a half bushels.

The cones are then dried and the seeds are removed in wind tunnels with huge fans. A bushel of cones will yield about ten ounces of seeds. In some years the seeds are large and will average 47,000 seeds per pound; in other years the seeds are small and will average as many as 99,000 seeds per pound. Both small and large seeds germinate at about the same rate. Black spruce cones often must be soaked in water, then dried in kilns before they will yield their seeds, which may amount to as many as half a million per pound.

Blue spruce seeds require no special treatment or storage other than to be kept dry and cool. Some seeds stored dry in sealed containers at temperatures just above freezing (36 to 40 degrees Fahrenheit) still have excellent viability after ten years.

Some seeds must be passed through the digestive system of birds before they will germinate and some must be heated by forest fires before the cones will release them. It is estimated by some tree specialists that ideal conditions for nature to reproduce a coniferous forest exist only rarely, perhaps for the sequoia as seldom as once in 10,000 years. Few people use a giant redwood for a Christmas tree, however!

Tree Species

Many species of spruce are used for Christmas trees. Territorial preference dictates which trees farmers grow. Some areas in New England are best suited to fir. Pine is popular throughout the Midwest.

Probably ten million of several varieties of Scotch pine are sold annually. Scotch pine lend themselves well to pruning and hold their needles a long time. Blue spruce retain their needles as well as pine and, in addition, have straighter stems and the natural color preferred by some tree buyers. Some spruce, such as the Engelmann spruce, yield well to the shaping shears and hold their needles a long time if harvested when temperatures are above freez-

ing. If they are cut in subfreezing weather, however, they will shed their needles in just a few days.

Many tree growers plant several varieties just for the joy of trying a new crop. Some growers also supply living trees to the landscape market—usually the runts of the Christmas tree crop. Runts are those trees that for genetic, site location, or some unknown reason do not develop into full-sized specimens.

Growing Seedlings

Few Christmas tree growers collect their own seed. Indeed, most tree growers do not even raise their own seedlings (plants grown in a seedbed). Seedlings removed from a seedbed and planted in rows or other beds are called transplants. Transplants are indicated by the terms 2-1 or 2-2, meaning they are two years old and transplanted one time (in the first example) or two years old and transplanted two times (in the second example). Such plants are used mostly by growers raising ornamental plants. Most Christmas tree farmers buy 2-0 seedlings from professional growers and transplant them in their own fields.

Spruce seedbeds are usually fall-planted, after being treated with a 5 percent sulfuric acid solution, in light sandy soil with good drainage. Seeds are often sown at a rate that will produce 75 plants per square foot. Each bed is usually about three or four feet wide and runs as long as the land allows.

Most seedlings are susceptible to several varieties of pre- and post-emergence fungi. Control of the fungi is achieved by decreasing available moisture or by spraying chemicals. Often, farmers raising tree stock will sow several varieties of seeds to reduce their risks in case one variety should for any number of reasons fail. These reasons might include birds or rodents ingesting the seeds, as well as any virus that might attack the trees. All the beds must be kept free of weeds so the desired plants can get the required amount of sun and water. Most seedling growers use chemicals for weed control and have irrigation systems to ensure adequate watering. Some tree seedlings require partial shade. It is not uncommon to see many rows of snow fence covering the tender conifer seedlings.

Colorado blue spruce seed will often germinate or sprout 10 to 30 days after planting. Plants for Christmas tree use are normally removed from the seedbeds in the spring following their second growing season. The plants at that time are perhaps six to twelve inches tall.

Seedlings are harvested by tractors pulling a blade ten or twelve inches below the surface of the ground. The blade extends across the entire seedbed. Often in the same operation the seedlings are lifted into racks that shake away the soil and the plants are collected into bundles as wide as a basketball. From the moment the plants are lifted from the ground, they are at risk. Only a few moments of hot sun or dry winds can kill the hairlike roots. Skilled operators keep recently lifted plants covered and transport them immediately to refrigerated storage facilities.

Small-scale tree farmers (those planting only a few thousand trees each spring) lucky enough to have a personal relationship with a seedling grower often pick up their plants the same day they are dug and thus avoid the refrigeration step in the harvest. Large-scale planters often plant 100,000 seedlings in one season and that amount of trees takes many hours of labor to lift, count, and bundle.

Transplanting

Christmas tree planting takes place in early spring during the brisk days of late March or the rainy days of early April when cold winds whistle around a planter's wet fingers.

Small-scale planters often prepare their field by plowing and tilling the soil one year prior to planting. This reduces the weed crop and thus the competition for sun and rain. It also facilitates harvest by making the land level and easy to work on. Other growers plow contoured single furrows perhaps six feet apart and plant the seedlings six feet apart in the bottom of the furrows. Some growers like wider spacing and plant 10 feet apart. At any rate, the furrow method places the plant in sterile soil and away from weed competition for the first few years. The furrow also serves to gather rainwater. But the plowed furrow method makes the harvesting of trees difficult. Cut-it-yourself customers and wholesalers prefer level land.

Some small-scale growers plant their seedlings in neat soldier-like rows, without disturbing the topsoil that has been exposed to winter's sun and wind.

Undisturbed soil grows fewer weeds. Large-scale growers often use a pre-emergence herbicide. Some small-scale growers plant grass seed between the rows of Christmas tree seedlings. Some even plant a few crocus! When the grass is mowed the plantation looks like a formal garden. Cut-it-yourself customers like to select a tree from a plantation that is free of briars, thistles, burrs, and saw-toothed grasses. Large-scale growers do not cater to cut-it-yourself customers and instead wholesale their trees to distributors, who sell to retailers, who maintain local tree lots.

Large-scale growers plant their seedlings with a planting machine. Often this machine is hauled by a tractor. Usually one person drives the tractor and two people ride on the tree planter. A rolling coulter (like a huge round pizza knife) opens the soil, and a double plowshare holds the soil apart long enough for the people planting to insert a seedling in the trench at regular intervals. Then the tree is packed into place by two wheels set far enough apart to straddle the seedling but close enough to compact the soil. A three-person crew working this way can plant thousands of trees in one day.

Small-scale growers usually use the spud method. Over the years a heavy steel, pointed tool has been developed. One considered close to ideal measures three inches wide and ten inches long. It is welded to a steel tube about two feet long. The tool has a crossbar at the top of the blade so the user can step on the tool and drive it into the ground. The tool also has a crossbar or handle at the top of the tube so the user can direct it into a desired location.

The user places the spud at a 30 degree angle about three inches in front of the desired location for the seedling, drives the spud into the

ground with his or her foot, straightens the spud to a vertical position and removes it from the ground. Another person inserts the seedling, first making certain the roots are straight down in the hole. Seedlings inserted with doubled over root systems will not prosper and may die. When the seedling is properly placed in the hole the person covering the plant inserts a spud about three inches in front of the hole and presses that soil against the seedling. As a final effort, one usually trods heavily on the soil around the seedling to make certain it is firmly packed.

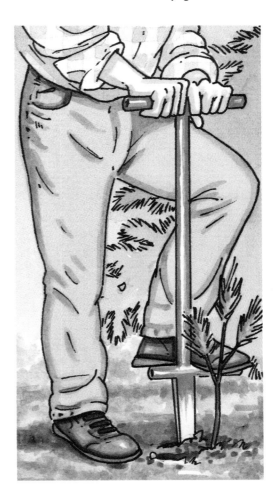

Irrigation

Trees that are properly chosen by species for the type of soil in which they are planted (pine in sand, spruce in heavy soil, fir on north slopes with air drainage) and that are watered by normal amounts of rain will grow and prosper without fertilization or irrigation. Most Christmas tree plantations are grown on land otherwise unsuitable for row crops or small grains. Christmas trees mature over such a long period of time (7 to 10 years for pine, 12 to 15 years for spruce) that irrigation costs would wipe out potential profits long before harvest. Few Christmas tree plantations are irrigated.

Weed Control

Weed control in a Christmas tree plantation is a must. A new conifer shoot can be killed by a mere blade of grass brushing against it often enough by the blowing wind. This is why natural conifer stands are never mixed with mature deciduous trees. This is also why a careful grounds-keeper keeps the lawnmower away from blue spruce.

Many growers, ever more conscious of pollutants, hesitate to use chemicals to control weeds. Still, for many growers, it is the only economical method of weed control available. Small-scale operators, by not charging their labor and wear-and-tear on their lawn mowers, keep level plantations weed-free by frequent mowing.

Growers who plant in the bottom of furrows often, to their dismay, soon find shoulder-high weeds growing in the disturbed soil above the furrow. The danger of the weeds is that they often become laden with snow in the winter and droop over onto the seedlings, sometimes smothering the plants by cutting off their light and air. Or they can provide shelter for mice, which may eat the bark, girdle the trunk, and kill the plant.

Small-scale growers who plant in the bottom of furrows sometimes walk through their plantation after the late autumn frosts and trod all weeds away from their seedlings. Although this is time-consuming, it is an effective way to help the plants through their first several winters.

Pest Control

Newly planted seedlings are seldom attacked by insects. But by their third or fourth year, insects that for decades have had no conifers to devour will find the plants and set to work on them.

Cultivated pine trees often are attacked by shoot moths. This moth lays its eggs in the base of the tender new growth of the plant. The egg hatches into a worm that eats the center of the new shoot until the shoot is unable to support its weight and becomes bent or twisted at odd angles. When this happens to enough new shoots the resulting tree is unsalable because Christmas tree customers prefer a tree that is symmetrical about the center line and conical, not bent and twisted.

Shoot moth is controllable only by chemicals. Helicopters are often used to apply insecticides, herbicides, and fungicides. Costs for the materials per acre are usually less than the expense of hiring the helicopter.

Most conifers are also attacked by sawfly, which lay many eggs that hatch into brownish-green worms about an inch long. Each worm will eat several new pine needles in a day. Within a week, untreated branches will be stripped bare by sawfly worms and the branch will die. The following year the entire tree may be attacked and may die. Small-scale growers can dislodge these worms from the branches by knocking them to the ground where they will perish. The worms will not climb back up the tree. But even small-scale growers can knock off only so many worms per day and thus they also usually resort to chemicals. Sawfly larvae usually need to be controlled from mid-May until early June. Tent caterpillars and webworms can also be a nuisance.

Special licenses are required to apply insect control substances. Many small-scale growers hire custom sprayers. Large-scale growers often do such custom spraying and usually own their own equipment.

Another threat to young trees is deer. Dozens of methods for keeping deer from sampling newly planted seedlings are on the market, but none are anywhere near 100 percent effective.

Pruning

By the time Christmas trees are knee-high they may grow so much in one season that a long gap exists between one year's growth and the next. Most Christmas tree customers prefer a dense plant, one through which the wall in back of the tree may not be seen and one from which ornaments may be uniformly displayed. To produce such a tree, growers must annually shape their plants. This operation is usually called pruning.

Large-scale and small-scale operations now assume equal footing as each tree must be hand-shaped. Some growers use machetes. Some use gasoline engine powered shears; some use battery power. Many use hedge shears. The first few years after planting, young trees need only the terminal shoot trimmed. Within a couple of years, however, the lateral shoots will need to be shortened also.

A natural shoot will normally produce between one and five buds for the next year's growth. A shoot that has been pruned will produce from five to a dozen buds. Thus, a pruned tree will be more dense than a tree that is not. A tree that is pruned severely at the base will grow slender and a tree that is not pruned at the base, or only pruned moderately, will be as wide or wider than it is high when it is six or seven feet tall and ready for harvest.

Most growers prune pine trees in late May or early June. Usually, a later pruning results in more insect control because the insect eggs laid in shoots are pruned away. While many growers prune spruce in the late spring, some prefer to begin this operation the day after Christmas. Winter pruning is particularly effective for Norway spruce. Blue spruce do not respond well to a knife. They are normally referred to as self-pruning but may require a wee nip here and there to remove a particularly offensive limb. The usual rule for pruning is, according to old-timers in the tree business, "better anytime than never."

Most state colleges distribute free literature on tree growing, including information on correct procedures for pruning. Many seedling growers also provide hints for growing trees. In general, one should prune away what is offensive; keep what is pleasing. The pruner looks at the tree and imagines what it could look like, then uses the hedge shears as an artist might use a brush.

Some small-scale growers work so hard and for so many years on a particular tree in an effort to make it salable, they become fond of it. Other growers claim plants react favorably when spoken to kindly. As some people may think this a bit odd, one who talks to plants should, perhaps, keep it a secret.

Ready for Sale

And so for the 12 to 15 years after planting, Christmas tree growers weed and prune and spray, pay ad valorem taxes, and wait for the crop. Some people say it is a waste to saw down a tree and use it for just a few days and then discard it. But it is for this reason the trees were grown; just as it is why poinsettias or Easter lilies or the flowers for a wedding bouquet are grown. During the lifetime of the tree plantation it may produce several tons of oxygen and accumulate perhaps a hundredth of an inch of humus beneath its limbs, thus enriching both the environments of air and soil in which it grows.

Wholesale buyers of Christmas trees at large-scale plantations take every usable tree the first year. Painful as it may be to learn, unsalable trees are bulldozed into a pile and burned. The land is then immediately prepared for another crop.

Small-scale growers may cut from a plantation for several years and endeavor to salvage trees initially considered by customers to be unsalable. Cut-it-yourself plantations may require five or six years before all the salable trees are sold, and a new plantation can be started.

Trees sold to wholesalers are often painted green in the last week of September. A large tanker truck will drive up and down on the fire lanes

(there is usually one every 20 rows) and from a long boom spray-paint the trees the color desired by the purchaser. Then in late October the trees are cut, run through a shaking machine to remove loose needles, bird nests, and broken twigs, then baled. The baling machine is not unlike a huge funnel. A cable is attached to the lower limb of the tree and it is pulled into the diminishing diameter of the funnel and wrapped in plastic netting much as a spider wraps a fly. This is done so that more trees per truck can be transported without damage. Some wholesalers have such a large operation that they cut trees year-round. They usually paint these trees and package them and store them a degree or two above freezing.

Only freezing rain discourages sales at a cut-it-yourself tree farm more than ordinary rain does. Few people have proper gear to harvest trees in the rain. A snowstorm, on the other hand, will bring out the Christmas spirit in even a Bah Humbugger. A light dusting of snow on the Friday after Thanksgiving is the best weather imaginable for a tree farmer. To many people, warm, sun-

ny December days and Christmas tree selection activities don't mix. Mostly, only the older folks come out on a nice day to get a tree. Perhaps that is because they remember those years when they selected a tree in inclement weather. Children don't care. They would come in a blizzard or during a tornado!

Some people come to the same tree farm year after year. Tree growers watch many a burgeoning family outgrow their first two-door sedan and fill to capacity an eight-passenger station wagon. They watch kids grow into responsible youths and come to select a tree for their church. They are invited to weddings and christenings. They are greeted year-round in stores and on the street by preschoolers as the Christmas-tree people. They glow inside.

As mentioned earlier, it is rare for all trees in a small-scale plantation to be sold the first or even the second year it is opened to the public. People like to have a large selection of goods from which to choose. Still, after customers can no longer find premium trees, some quality trees, at least in the grower's estimation, will remain. But finally, a tree farmer must accept the fact that not every item produced in a given endeavor will appeal to a potential buyer. The few remaining trees must be cleared away so that a new crop of seedlings may be planted. All this is done in anticipation of many more Christmases yet to come.

A Perfect Gift

JUNE KENNEDY MCLANE

I SAT IN THE CIRCLE of warmth of the wood stove in the kitchen on that December evening and talked happily of the books, paper, and box of paints I hoped to find under the tree on Christmas morning. Dad lay his book aside and got up from his rocking chair to lay another chunk of wood onto the dying embers of the fire.

"There won't be a Christmas this year," he said.

Chastened, I stopped my chatter. I was a little afraid of Dad. This grim, silent man was a stranger to me. Why didn't he smile anymore? It seemed a long time since he had played games with me, laughing joyously at my nonsense. But no Christmas? Surely Dad was teasing me, but I was afraid in my heart that he meant what he said.

Dad and I had only each other now and, though I was only ten, I knew the reason we had moved during the middle of the night to this small house in the country. There was back rent due on the house in town and Dad was out of work. He sold the eggs from our pitifully small flock of chickens, which somehow kept us alive.

One of my chores was to feed the chickens. I was terrified of the hens and they knew it. One loose-looking hen with mean yellow eyes ruffled her feathers into an untidy heap and hurled herself at me every time I came near. If I didn't get out of the chicken yard fast enough, she pecked viciously at my legs. I hated that hen. I named her Lizzie, the ugliest name I knew. I dreamed of the day we would be rich and I wouldn't have to feed chickens anymore.

On the morning of Christmas Eve, after the breakfast dishes were washed and put away, I swept the floor, shook out the rag rug that lay beneath Dad's rocking chair, and straightened the pile of books that lay on the table. I hoped Dad would be pleased. Taking a deep breath, I asked if we might bake Christmas cookies. Dad stood wordless for a long moment. Suddenly I found it hard to swallow. What had I done? I hung my head and waited for whatever he would say. With a gentleness that surprised me, he asked, "Girl, does Christmas really mean so much to you?" and turned away when I couldn't answer.

I was subdued the rest of the morning, but I was not as quiet as Dad. He was more withdrawn than usual, not hearing when I spoke to him. After our noon bowl of soup, he put on his mackinaw, pulled his stocking cap close around his ears, and searched his pockets for his mittens.

"I have something to do," he said. "You stay inside where it's warm. Mind the fire and don't worry about the chickens, I'll feed them while I'm out." At the door he turned. "I'll be a while," he added.

Dad was gone for a very long time. I spent anxious moments at the window wondering where he had gone and watching for his return. The view from the window was far from heartening. The ruts in the lane were frozen iron hard. The weeds in the fields bowed almost to the ground in submission to the bitter wind's urging. Two crows flapped their way across the leaden sky to the shelter of the woods beyond. It was beginning to snow.

The afternoon faded into evening and there was still no sign of Dad. I lighted the oil lamp, being careful not to smudge the glass chimney. I looked again at the red and gold foil bookmarks made from the envelope liners from my box of treasures. The bookmarks were for Dad's Christmas present. He loved to read, and usually marked his page with a broom straw or a scrap of paper. I sighed as I put the gaily colored papers into Dad's book, wondering if he would ever see them. What would I do if Dad never came back and I was left alone? Would the landlord put me out? I remembered my favorite story of the little match girl who had no place to go and who tried to keep warm on a winter's night by lighting her matches, one by one. I cried every time I read the story.

I could see the big box of blue-headed safety matches on the shelf above the stove. It was almost full, but how long would the box of matches keep me warm? I could see myself standing by the corner of the chicken shed, lighting my matches and hoping that Clem Armstrong would drive by with his team. His heart would melt at my plight and he would take me home to live with his family.

In my fantasy, the cruel wind blew out my last match before Clem came along. Tears stung my ears. I would die there by the chicken shed and only mean old Lizzie would know what had happened. She would smile a gloating chicken smile. Clem would find my poor, starved body and be sorry. I was trying to decide what came next when I heard the longed-for steps on the porch. Dad was home!

Dad tottered in stiff legged and pinched with cold. In his arms he carried a small pine tree. The tree was freshly cut and its sharp fragrance filled the kitchen. Dad moved close to the warmth of the stove, rubbing his hands and stamping his feet to encourage circulation.

"Do you think you can trim this tree for Christmas?" he asked.

My heart gave a joyful leap. I knew Christmas would come if I had faith, as they said in church. Christmas would come if I *believed*.

I spent the evening making paper chains to adorn our tree. That night, I curled under my blankets and let my mind roam freely to last Christmas Eve when Mama worked in a kitchen fragrant with the warm smells of baking. I remembered again the beautiful Christmas tree trimmed with lights and tinsel and banked with packages. There would be packages this year, too, I told myself. Why else would Dad have brought a Christmas tree if there weren't to be gifts?

I woke with eager anticipation the next morning and hurried to the kitchen to dress next to the warmth of the stove. I tried not to look at the space beneath the tree but my eyes betrayed me, moving of their own accord. There were no packages under the tree, no book, no watercolor paints. There was *nothing* there. My face felt stiff, too frozen even for tears.

"How about pancakes and jam this morning?" Dad asked, remembering my favorite breakfast. Not looking at him, I nodded dumbly. Somehow I ate my breakfast. If there was jam on my pancakes, I didn't notice. I was stacking the dishes when Dad said, "Close your eyes and hold out your hands. I have a surprise."

I squeezed my eyes tight and held my hands before me, hope again rising in my heart. "Please, oh please, God," I prayed. "A book is enough, let it be a book. I'll be good from now on and Dad won't have to scold me for not cleaning the lamp chimneys." Something clammy cold was placed in my hands before I could finish my prayer. I shrank back with a small cry and opened my eyes. I held a cold, dead chicken. There were small holes in the skin where the feathers had been plucked. The blue muscles of the legs showed through the whitish yellow skin. The neck dangled and a drop of dark blood remained on the headless stump. I looked at Dad. There was a pleading look in his eyes.

"We'll have chicken for dinner today," he said. "For Christmas." In spite of my disappointment, I recognized in another human being a need even greater than my own.

"Oh yes, Dad," I babbled. "We can each have a drumstick." A rare smile lit his face. I looked at my hands, afraid of crying. How could Dad imagine that a dead chicken was a gift? I longed for something wrapped in tissue paper and tied with ribbon. A thought struck me.

"Which chicken was it, Dad?"

"Lizzie," he said. I swallowed. Hated Lizzie, our best laying hen. Perfect gifts come in many guises.

Lizzie's flesh was toothsome and her broth made rich, golden gravy to pour over the biscuits Dad made. After dinner, he pulled the rocking chair close to the stove and I sat on his lap. He held me close while he read aloud, and when he finished reading he marked his place with a red foil bookmark. I found that I didn't mind the absence of gifts, after all. I had my father back.

Dad never told me where he cut the little pine tree to try to give me Christmas. I knew the fields and woods around our home with the thoroughness of an inquisitive ten-year-old. There were oak, hickory, black walnut, maple, and sumac trees, but there were no pines. Was the tree yet another Christmas miracle?

Our Christmas

Christmas Eve _____
_____
_____

Christmas Day _____
_____
_____

Christmas Worship _____
_____
_____

Christmas
Photo

Christmas Guests   Christmas Gifts
_____   _____
_____   _____
_____   _____
_____   _____

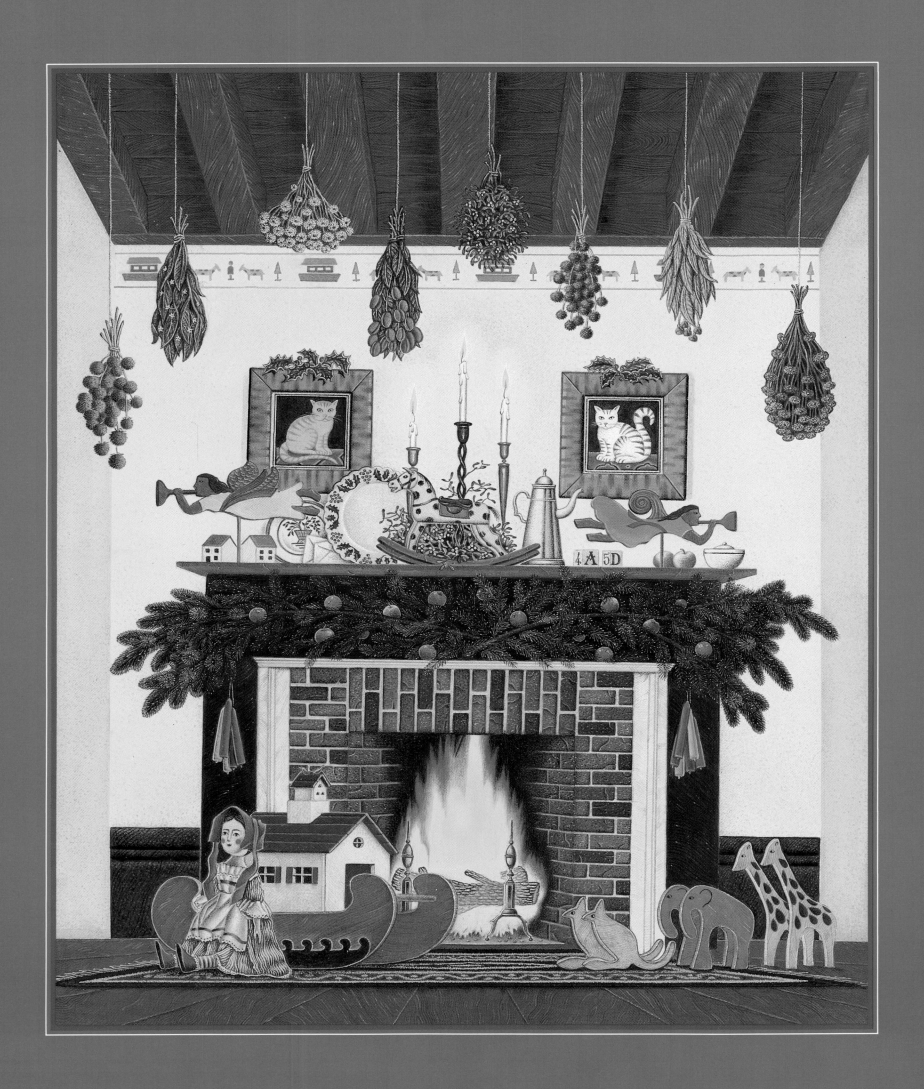